Techniques of the Observer

On Vision and Modernity in the Nineteenth Century

JONATHAN CRARY

An OCTOBER *Book*

MIT Press
Cambridge, Massachusetts
London, England

Second printing, 1991
©1990 Massachusetts Institute of Technology

This book was set in ITC Garamond by DEKR Corp. and printed and bound by Halliday
Lithograph in the United States of America.

Library of Congress Cataloging-in-Publication Data

Crary, Jonathan.
  Techniques of the observer : on vision and modernity in the
  nineteenth century / Jonathan Crary.
    p.   cm.
  "October books"—Ser. t.p.
  Includes bibliographical references (p.
  ISBN 0-262-03169-8
  1. Visual perception. 2. Art, Modern—19th century—Themes,
motives. 3. Art and society—History—19th century. I. Title.
N7430.5.C7   1990
701'.15—dc20
                                                            90-6164
                                                            CIP
Illustration credits: Musée du Louvre, Paris (page 44); Städelsches Kunstinstitut,
Frankfurt (page 45); Museo Correr, Venice (page 53); The National Gallery, London
(page 54); private collection, Paris, photo by Lauros-Giraudon (page 63); National Gallery of Art, Washington (page 65); photos by L. L. Roger-Viollet (pages 117, 123, 130);
Tate Gallery, London (pages 140, 144).

to my father

Contents

Acknowledgments

Among the people who made this book possible are my three friends and colleagues at *Zone* Sanford Kwinter, Hal Foster, and Michel Feher. It would be impossible to suggest all the ways in which I have been enriched and challenged because of my proximity to their work and ideas. I would also like to thank Richard Brilliant and David Rosand for their consistent support and encouragement, especially when these were needed most. Their counsel was invaluable to me during the formulation of this project. I am particularly grateful to Rosalind Krauss for her discerning critical suggestions and help of many kinds. Yve-Alain Bois and Christopher Phillips read early versions of the manuscript and made probing and highly useful observations. I did much of my research while the recipient of a Rudolf Wittkower Fellowship from the Columbia Art History Department. The book was completed while I was on a Mellon Fellowship in the Society of Fellows in the Humanities at Columbia, and thanks go to my friends at the Heyman Center during that time. In preparing the visual material I relied on the assistance of Meighan Gale, Anne Mensior of CLAM, and Greg Schmitz. Ted Byfield and my research assistant Lynne Spriggs provided last-minute editorial help. Finally, I would like to thank Suzanne Jackson, whose commitment and risk taking as a writer continually stimulated and strengthened my own work.

Techniques of the Observer

For the materialist historian, every epoch with which he occupies himself is only a fore-history of that which really concerns him. And that is precisely why the appearance of repetition doesn't exist for him in history, because the moments in the course of history which matter most to him become moments of the present through their index as "fore-history," and change their characteristics according to the catastrophic or triumphant determination of that present.

— Walter Benjamin, *Arcades Project*

1   Modernity and the Problem of the Observer

> *The field of vision has always seemed to me comparable to the ground of an archaeological excavation.*
>
> —Paul Virilio

This is a book about vision and its historical construction. Although it primarily addresses events and developments before 1850, it was written in the midst of a transformation in the nature of visuality probably more profound than the break that separates medieval imagery from Renaissance perspective. The rapid development in little more than a decade of a vast array of computer graphics techniques is part of a sweeping reconfiguration of relations between an observing subject and modes of representation that effectively nullifies most of the culturally established meanings of the terms *observer* and *representation*. The formalization and diffusion of computer-generated imagery heralds the ubiquitous implantation of fabricated visual "spaces" radically different from the mimetic capacities of film, photography, and television. These latter three, at least until the mid-1970s, were generally forms of analog media that still corresponded to the optical wavelengths of the spectrum and to a point of view, static or mobile, located in real space. Computer-aided design, synthetic holography, flight simulators, computer animation, robotic image recognition, ray tracing, texture mapping, motion control, virtual environment helmets, magnetic resonance imaging, and multispectral sensors are only a few of the techniques that are relocating vision to a plane severed from a human observer. Obviously other older and more familiar modes of "seeing" will persist and coexist uneasily alongside these new forms. But increasingly these emergent technologies of image production are becoming the dominant models of visualization according to which primary social processes and institutions function. And, of course, they are intertwined with the needs of global information industries and with the expanding requirements of medical, military, and police hierarchies. Most of the historically important functions of the human eye are being supplanted by practices in which visual images no longer have any reference to the position of an observer in a "real," optically perceived world. If these images can be said to refer to anything, it is to millions of bits of electronic mathematical data. Increasingly, visuality will be situated on a cybernetic and electromagnetic terrain where abstract visual and linguistic elements coincide and are consumed, circulated, and exchanged globally.

To comprehend this relentless abstraction of the visual and to avoid mystifying it by recourse to technological explanations, many questions would have to be posed and answered. Some of the most crucial of these questions are historical. If there is in fact an ongoing mutation in the nature of visuality, what forms or modes are being left behind? What kind of break is it? At the same time, what are the elements of continuity that link contemporary imagery with older organizations of the visual? To what extent, if at all, are computer graphics and the contents of the video display terminal a further elaboration and refinement of what Guy Debord designated as the "society of the spectacle?"[1] What is the relation between the dematerialized digital imagery of the present and the so-called age of mechanical reproduction? The most urgent questions, though, are larger ones. How is the body, including the observing body, becoming a component of new machines, economies, apparatuses, whether social, libidinal, or technological? In what ways is subjectivity becoming a precarious condition of interface between rationalized systems of exchange and networks of information?

Although this book does not directly engage these questions, it attempts to reconsider and reconstruct part of their historical background. It does this by studying an earlier reorganization of vision in the first half of the nine-

---

1.   See my "Eclipse of the Spectacle," in *Art After Modernism: Rethinking Representation,* ed. Brian Wallis (Boston, 1984), pp. 283–294.

teenth century, sketching out some of the events and forces, especially in the 1820s and 1830s, that produced a new kind of observer and that were crucial preconditions for the ongoing abstraction of vision outlined above. Although the immediate cultural repercussions of this reorganization were less dramatic, they were nonetheless profound. Problems of vision then, as now, were fundamentally questions about the body and the operation of social power. Much of this book will examine how, beginning early in the nineteenth century, a new set of relations between the body on one hand and forms of institutional and discursive power on the other redefined the status of an observing subject.

By outlining some of the "points of emergence" of a modern and heterogeneous regime of vision, I simultaneously address the related problem of when, and because of what events, there was a rupture with Renaissance, or *classical,* models of vision and of the observer. How and where one situates such a break has an enormous bearing on the intelligibility of visuality within nineteenth- and twentieth-century modernity. Most existing answers to this question suffer from an exclusive preoccupation with problems of visual *representation;* the break with classical models of vision in the early nineteenth century was far more than simply a shift in the appearance of images and art works, or in systems of representational conventions. Instead, it was inseparable from a massive reorganization of knowledge and social practices that modified in myriad ways the productive, cognitive, and desiring capacities of the human subject.

In this study I present a relatively unfamiliar configuration of nineteenth-century objects and events, that is, proper names, bodies of knowledge, and technological inventions that rarely appear in histories of art or of modernism. One reason for doing this is to escape from the limitations of many of the dominant histories of visuality in this period, to bypass the many accounts of modernism and modernity that depend on a more or less similar evaluation of the origins of modernist visual art and culture in the 1870s and 1880s. Even today, with numerous revisions and rewritings (including some of the most compelling neo-Marxist, feminist, and poststructuralist work), a core narrative remains essentially unchanged. It goes something like the following: with Manet, impressionism, and/or postimpressionism, a new model of visual representation and perception emerges that constitutes a break with several centuries of another model of vision, loosely definable as Renaissance, perspectival, or normative. Most theories of modern visual culture are still bound to one or other version of this "rupture."

Yet this narrative of the end of perspectival space, of mimetic codes, and of the referential has usually coexisted uncritically with another very different periodization of the history of European visual culture that equally needs to be abandoned. This second model concerns the invention and dissemination of photography and other related forms of "realism" in the nineteenth century. Overwhelmingly, these developments have been presented as part of the continuous unfolding of a Renaissance-based mode of vision in which photography, and eventually cinema, are simply later instances of an ongoing deployment of perspectival space and perception. Thus we are often left with a confusing bifurcated model of vision in the nineteenth century: on one level there is a relatively small number of advanced artists who generated a radically new kind of seeing and signification, while on a more quotidian level vision remains embedded within the same general "realist" strictures that had organized it since the fifteenth century. Classical space is overturned, so it seems, on one hand, but persists on the other. This conceptual division leads to the erroneous notion that something called realism dominated popular representational practices, while experiments and innovations occurred in a distinct (if often permeable) arena of modernist art making.

When examined closely, however, the celebrated "rupture" of modernism is considerably more restricted in its cultural and social impact than the fanfare surrounding it usually suggests. The alleged perceptual revolution of advanced art in the late nineteenth century, according to its proponents, is an event whose effects occur *outside* the most dominant and pervasive modes of seeing. Thus, following the logic of this general argument, it is actually a rupture that occurs on the margins of a vast hegemonic organization of the visual that becomes increasingly powerful in the twentieth century, with the diffusion and proliferation of photography, film, and television. In a sense, however, the myth of modernist rupture depends fundamentally on the binary model of realism vs. experimentation. That is, the essential continuity of mimetic codes is a necessary condition for the affirmation of an avant-garde breakthrough. The notion of a modernist visual revolution depends on the presence of a subject with a detached viewpoint, from which modernism—

whether as a style, as cultural resistance, or as ideological practice—can be isolated against the background of a normative vision. Modernism is thus presented as the appearance of the new for an observer who remains perpetually the same, or whose historical status is never interrogated.

It is not enough to attempt to describe a dialectical relation between the innovations of avant-garde artists and writers in the late nineteenth century and the concurrent "realism" and positivism of scientific and popular culture. Rather, it is crucial to see both of these phenomena as overlapping components of a single social surface on which the modernization of vision had begun decades earlier. I am suggesting here that a broader and far more important transformation in the makeup of vision occurred in the early nineteenth century. Modernist painting in the 1870s and 1880s and the development of photography after 1839 can be seen as later symptoms or consequences of this crucial systemic shift, which was well under way by 1820.

But, one may ask at this point, doesn't the history of art effectively coincide with a history of perception? Aren't the changing forms of artworks over time the most compelling record of how vision itself has mutated historically? This study insists that, on the contrary, a history of vision (if such is even possible) depends on far more than an account of shifts in representational practices. What this book takes as its object is not the empirical data of artworks or the ultimately idealist notion of an isolable "perception," but instead the no less problematic phenomenon of the observer. For the problem of the observer is the field on which vision in history can be said to materialize, to become itself visible. Vision and its effects are always inseparable from the possibilities of an observing subject who is both the historical product *and* the site of certain practices, techniques, institutions, and procedures of subjectification.

Most dictionaries make little semantic distinction between the words "observer" and "spectator," and common usage usually renders them effectively synonomous. I have chosen the term *observer* mainly for its etymological resonance. Unlike *spectare,* the Latin root for "spectator," the root for "observe" does not literally mean "to look at." Spectator also carries specific connotations, especially in the context of nineteenth-century culture, that I prefer to avoid—namely, of one who is a passive onlooker at a spectacle, as at an art gallery or theater. In a sense more pertinent to my study, *observare* means "to conform one's action, to comply with," as in observing rules, codes, regulations, and practices. Though obviously one who sees, an observer is more importantly one who sees within a prescribed set of possibilities, one who is embedded in a system of conventions and limitations. And by "conventions" I mean to suggest far more than representational practices. If it can be said there is an observer specific to the nineteenth century, or to any period, it is only as an *effect* of an irreducibly heterogeneous system of discursive, social, technological, and institutional relations. There is no observing subject prior to this continually shifting field.[2]

If I have mentioned the idea of a history of vision, it is only as a hypothetical possibility. Whether perception or vision actually change is irrelevant, for they have no autonomous history. What changes are the plural forces and rules composing the field in which perception occurs. And what determines vision at any given historical moment is not some deep structure, economic base, or world view, but rather the functioning of a collective assemblage of disparate parts on a single social surface. It may even be necessary to consider the observer as a distribution of events located in many different places.[3] There never was or will be a self-present beholder to whom a world is transparently evident. Instead there are more or less powerful arrangements of forces out of which the capacities of an observer are possible.

In proposing that during the first few decades of the nineteenth century a new kind of observer took shape in Europe radically different from the type of observer dominant in the seventeenth and eighteenth centuries, I doubtless provoke the question of how one can pose such large generalities, such

2.   In one sense, my aims in this study are "genealogical," following Michel Foucault: "I don't believe the problem can be solved by historicizing the subject as posited by the phenomenologists, fabricating a subject that evolves through the course of history. One has to dispense with the constituent subject, to get rid of the subject itself, that's to say, to arrive at an analysis which can account for the constitution of the subject within a historical framework. And this is what I would call genealogy, that is, a form of history which can account for the constitution of knowledges, discourses, domains of objects, etc., without having to make reference to a subject which is either transcendental in relation to a field of events or runs in its empty sameness throughout the course of history." *Power/Knowledge* (New York, 1980), p. 117.

3.   On scientific and intellectual traditions in which objects "are aggregrates of relatively independent parts," see Paul Feyerabend, *Problems of Empiricism,* vol. 2 (Cambridge, 1981), p. 5.

unqualified categories as "the observer in the nineteenth century." Doesn't this risk presenting something abstracted and divorced from the singularities and immense diversity that characterized visual experience in that century? Obviously there was no single nineteenth-century observer, no example that can be located empirically. What I want to do, however, is suggest some of the conditions and forces that defined or allowed the formation of a dominant model of what an observer was in the nineteenth century. This will involve sketching out a set of related events that produced crucial ways in which vision was discussed, controlled, and incarnated in cultural and scientific practices. At the same time I hope to show how the major terms and elements of a previous organization of the observer were no longer in operation. What is *not* addressed in this study are the marginal and local forms by which dominant practices of vision were resisted, deflected, or imperfectly constituted. The history of such oppositional moments needs to be written, but it only becomes legible against the more hegemonic set of discourses and practices in which vision took shape. The typologies, and provisional unities that I use are part of an explanatory strategy for demonstrating a general break or discontinuity at the beginning of the nineteenth century. It should not be necessary to point out there are no such things as continuities and discontinuities in history, only in historical explanation. So my broad temporalizing is not in the interest of a "true history," or of restoring to the record "what actually happened." The stakes are quite different: how one periodizes and where one locates ruptures or denies them are all political choices that determine the construction of the present. Whether one excludes or foregrounds certain events and processes at the expense of others affects the intelligibility of the contemporary functioning of power in which we ourselves are enmeshed. Such choices affect whether the shape of the present seems "natural" or whether its historically fabricated and densely sedimented makeup is made evident.

In the early nineteenth century there was a sweeping transformation in the way in which an observer was figured in a wide range of social practices and domains of knowledge. A main path along which I present these developments is by examining the significance of certain optical devices. I discuss them not for the models of representation they imply, but as sites of both knowledge and power that operate directly on the body of the individual. Specifically, I pose the camera obscura as paradigmatic of the dominant status of the observer in the seventeenth and eighteenth centuries, while for the nineteenth century I discuss a number of optical instruments, in particular the stereoscope, as a means of detailing the observer's transformed status. The optical devices in question, most significantly, are points of intersection where philosophical, scientific, and aesthetic discourses overlap with mechanical techniques, institutional requirements, and socioeconomic forces. Each of them is understandable not simply as the material object in question, or as part of a history of technology, but for the way in which it is embedded in a much larger assemblage of events and powers. Clearly, this is to counter many influential accounts of the history of photography and cinema that are characterized by a latent or explicit technological determinism, in which an independent dynamic of mechanical invention, modification, and perfection imposes itself onto a social field, transforming it from the outside. On the contrary, technology is always a concomitant or subordinate part of other forces. For Gilles Deleuze, "A society is defined by its amalgamations, not by its tools . . . tools exist only in relation to the interminglings they make possible or that make them possible."[4] The point is that a history of the observer is not reducible to changing technical and mechanical practices any more than to the changing forms of artworks and visual representation. At the same time I would stress that even though I designate the camera obscura as a key object in the seventeenth and eighteenth centuries, it is not isomorphic to the optical techniques I discuss in the context of the nineteenth century. The eighteenth and nineteenth centuries are not analagous grids on which different cultural objects can occupy the same relative positions. Rather, the position and function of a technique is historically variable; the camera obscura, as I suggest in the next chapter, is part of a field of knowledge and practice that does not correspond structurally to the sites of the optical devices I examine subsequently. In Deleuze's words, "On one hand, each stratum or historical formation implies a distribution of the visible and the articulable which acts upon itself; on the other, from one stratum to the next there is a variation in the distri-

4.　　　Gilles Deleuze and Félix Guattari, *A Thousand Plateaus: Capitalism and Schizophrenia,* trans. Brian Massumi (Minneapolis, 1987), p. 90.

bution because the visibility itself changes in style while the statements themselves change their system."[5]

I argue that some of the most pervasive means of producing "realistic"
effects in mass visual culture, such as the stereoscope, were in fact based on
a radical abstraction and reconstruction of optical experience, thus demand-
ing a reconsideration of what "realism" means in the nineteenth century. I also
hope to show how the most influential figurations of an observer in the early
nineteenth century depended on the priority of models of subjective vision,
in contrast to the pervasive suppression of subjectivity in vision in seven-
teenth- and eighteenth-century thought. A certain notion of "subjective vision"
has long been a part of discussions of nineteenth-century culture, most often
in the context of Romanticism, for example in mapping out a shift in "the role
played by the mind in perception," from conceptions of imitation to ones of
expression, from metaphor of the mirror to that of the lamp.[6] But central to
such explanations is again the idea of a vision or perception that was somehow
unique to artists and poets, that was distinct from a vision shaped by empiricist
or positivist ideas and practices.

I am interested in the way in which concepts of subjective vision, of the
productivity of the observer, pervaded not only areas of art and literature but
were present in philosophical, scientific, and technological discourses. Rather
than stressing the separation between art and science in the nineteenth century, it is important to see how they were both part of a single interlocking
field of knowledge and practice. The same knowledge that allowed the
increasing rationalization and control of the human subject in terms of new
institutional and economic requirements was also a condition for new experiments in visual representation. Thus I want to delineate an observing subject
who was both a product of and at the same time constitutive of modernity in
the nineteenth century. Very generally, what happens to the observer in the
nineteenth century is a process of modernization; he or she is made adequate
to a constellation of new events, forces, and institutions that together are
loosely and perhaps tautologically definable as "modernity."

5.   Gilles Deleuze, *Foucault,* trans. Seán Hand (Minneapolis, 1988), p. 48.
6.   M. H. Abrams, *The Mirror and the Lamp: Romantic Theory and the Critical Tradition*
(London, 1953), pp. 57-65.

Modernization becomes a useful notion when extracted from teleological and primarily economic determinations, and when it encompasses not only structural changes in political and economic formations but also the immense reorganization of knowledge, languages, networks of spaces and communications, and subjectivity itself. Moving out from the work of Weber, Lukács, Simmel, and others, and from all the theoretical reflection spawned by the terms "rationalization" and "reification," it is possible to pose a logic of modernization that is radically severed from the idea of progress or development, and that entails nonlinear transformations. For Gianni Vattimo, modernity has precisely these "post-historical" features, in which the continual production of the new is what allows things to stay the same.[7] It is a logic of the same, however, that exists in inverse relation to the stability of traditional forms. Modernization is a process by which capitalism uproots and makes mobile that which is grounded, clears away or obliterates that which impedes circulation, and makes exchangeable what is singular.[8] This applies as much to bodies, signs, images, languages, kinship relations, religious practices, and nationalities as it does to commodities, wealth, and labor power. Modernization becomes a ceaseless and self-perpetuating creation of new needs, new consumption, and new production.[9] Far from being exterior to this process, the observer as human subject is completely immanent to it. Over the course

7.   Gianni Vattimo, *The End of Modernity,* trans. Jon R. Snyder (Baltimore, 1988), pp. 7–8.
8.   Relevant here is the historical outline in Gilles Deleuze and Félix Guattari, *Anti-Oedipus: Capitalism and Schizophrenia,* trans. Robert Hurley et. al., (New York, 1978), pp. 200–261. Here modernity is a continual process of "deterritorialization," a making abstract and interchangeable of bodies, objects, and relations. But, as Deleuze and Guattari insist, the new exchangeability of forms under capitalism is the condition for their "re-territorialization" into new hierarchies and institutions. Nineteenth-century industrialization is discussed in terms of deterritorialization, uprooting (*déracinement*), and the production of flows in Marc Guillaume, *Eloge du désordre* (Paris, 1978), pp. 34–42.
9.   See Karl Marx, *Grundrisse,* trans. Martin Nicolaus (New York, 1973), pp. 408–409: "Hence exploration of all nature in order to discover new, useful qualities in things; universal exchange of the products of all alien climates and lands; new (artificial) preparation of natural objects, by which they are given new use values. The exploration of the earth in all directions, to discover new things of use as well as new useful qualities of the old; . . . likewise the discovery, creation and satisfaction of new needs arising from society itself; the cultivation of all the qualities of the social human being, production of the same in a form as rich as possible in needs, because rich in qualities and relations—production of this being as the most total and universal possible social product."

of the nineteenth century, an observer increasingly had to function within disjunct and defamiliarized urban spaces, the perceptual and temporal dislocations of railroad travel, telegraphy, industrial production, and flows of typographic and visual information. Concurrently, the discursive identity of the observer as an object of philosophical reflection and empirical study underwent an equally drastic renovation.

The early work of Jean Baudrillard details some of the conditions of this new terrain in which a nineteenth-century observer was situated. For Baudrillard, one of the crucial consequences of the bourgeois political revolutions at the end of the 1700s was the ideological force that animated the myths of the rights of man, the right to equality and to happiness. In the nineteenth century, for the first time, observable proof became needed in order to demonstrate that happiness and equality had in fact been attained. Happiness had to be "*measurable* in terms of objects and signs," something that would be evident to the eye in terms of "*visible* criteria."[10] Several decades earlier, Walter Benjamin had also written about the role of the commodity in generating a "phantasmagoria of equality." Thus modernity is inseparable from on one hand a remaking of the observer, and on the other a proliferation of circulating signs and objects whose effects coincide with their visuality, or what Adorno calls *Anschaulichkeit*.[11]

Baudrillard's account of modernity outlines an increasing destabilization and mobility of signs and codes beginning in the Renaissance, signs previously rooted to relatively secure positions within fixed social hierarchies.

> There is no such thing as fashion in a society of caste and rank,
> since one is assigned a place irrevocably. Thus class mobility is
> non-existent. An interdiction protects the signs and assures them

10. Jean Baudrillard, *La société de consommation* (Paris, 1970), p. 60. Emphasis in original. Some of these changes have been described by Adorno as "the adaptation [of the observer] to the order of bourgeois rationality and, ultimately, the age of advanced industry, which was made by the eye when it accustomed itself to perceiving reality as a reality of objects and hence basically of commodities." *In Search of Wagner,* trans. Rodney Livingstone (London, 1981), p. 99.
11. Theodor Adorno, *Aesthetic Theory,* trans. C. Lenhardt (London, 1984), pp. 139–140: "By denying the implicitly conceptual nature of art, the norm of visuality reifies visuality into an opaque, impenetrable quality—a replica of the petrified world outside, wary of everything that might interfere with the pretence of the harmony the work puts forth."

a total clarity; each sign refers unequivocally to a status. . . . In caste societies, feudal or archaic, cruel societies, the signs are limited in number, and are not widely diffused, each one functions with its full value as interdiction, each is a reciprocal obligation between castes, clans, or persons. The signs are therefore anything but arbitrary. The arbitrary sign begins when, instead of linking two rsons in an unbreakable reciprocity, the signifier starts referring back to the disenchanted world of the signified, a common denominator of the real world to which no one has any obligation.[12]

Thus for Baudrillard modernity is bound up in the capacity of newly empowered social classes and groups to overcome the "exclusiveness of signs" and to initiate "a proliferation of signs on demand." Imitations, copies, counterfeits, and the techniques to produce them (which would include the Italian theater, linear perspective, and the camera obscura) were all challenges to the aristocratic monopoly and control of signs. The problem of mimesis here is not one of aesthetics but of social power, a power founded on the capacity to produce equivalences.

For Baudrillard and many others, however, it is clearly in the nineteenth century, alongside the development of new industrial techniques and new forms of political power, that a new kind of sign emerges. These new signs, "potentially indentical objects produced in indefinite series," herald the moment when the problem of mimesis disappears.

The relation between them [identical objects] is no longer that of an original to its counterfeit. The relation is neither analogy nor reflection, but equivalence and indifference. In a series, objects become undefined simulacra of each other. . . . We know now that is on the level of reproduction, of fashion, media, advertising, information, and communication (what Marx called the unessential sectors of capitalism) . . . that is to say in the sphere of the simulacra and the code, that the global process of capital is held together.[13]

12.   Jean Baudrillard, *L'échange symbolique et la mort* (Paris, 1976), p. 78; *Simulations,* trans. Paul Foss (New York, 1983), pp. 84–85.
13.   Baudrillard, *L'échange symbolique et la mort,* p. 86.

Within this new field of serially produced objects, the most significant, in terms of their social and cultural impact, were photography and a host of related techniques for the industrialization of image making.[14] The photograph becomes a central element not only in a new commodity economy but in the reshaping of an entire territory on which signs and images, each effectively severed from a referent, circulate and proliferate. Photographs may have some apparent similarities with older types of images, such as perspectival painting or drawings made with the aid of a camera obscura; but the vast systemic rupture of which photography is a part renders such similarities insignificant. Photography is an element of a new and homogeneous terrain of consumption and circulation in which an observer becomes lodged. To understand the "photography effect" in the nineteenth century, one must see it as a crucial component of a new cultural economy of value and exchange, not as part of a continuous history of visual representation.

Photography and money become homologous forms of social power in the nineteenth century.[15] They are equally totalizing systems for binding and unifying all subjects within a single global network of valuation and desire. As Marx said of money, photography is also a great leveler, a democratizer, a "mere symbol," a fiction "sanctioned by the so-called universal consent of mankind."[16] Both are magical forms that establish a new set of abstract relations between individuals and things and impose those relations as the real. It is through the distinct but interpenetrating economies of money and photography that a whole social world is represented and constituted exclusively as signs.

Photography, however, is not the subject of this book. Crucial as photography may be to the fate of visuality in the nineteenth century and beyond,

14.   The most important model for serial industrial production in the nineteenth century was ammunition and military spare parts. That the need for absolute similarity and exchangeability came out of the requirements of warfare, not out of developments in an economic sector, is argued in Manuel De Landa, *War in the Age of Intelligent Machines* (New York, 1990).
15.   For related arguments, see John Tagg, "The Currency of the Photograph," in *Thinking Photography,* ed. Victor Burgin (London, 1982), pp. 110–141; and Alan Sekula, "The Traffic in Photographs," in *Photography Against the Grain: Essays and Photo Works 1973– 1983* (Halifax, 1984), pp. 96–101.
16.   Karl Marx, *Capital,* vol. 1, trans. Samuel Moore and Edward Aveling (New York, 1967). p. 91.

its invention is secondary to the events I intend to detail here. My contention is that a reorganization of the observer occurs in the nineteenth century before the appearance of photography. What takes place from around 1810 to 1840 is an uprooting of vision from the stable and fixed relations incarnated in the camera obscura. If the camera obscura, as a concept, subsisted as an objective ground of visual truth, a variety of discourses and practices—in philosophy, science, and in procedures of social normalization—tend to abolish the foundations of that ground in the early nineteenth century. In a sense, what occurs is a new valuation of visual experience: it is given an unprecendented mobility and exchangeability, abstracted from any founding site or referent.

In chapter 3, I describe certain aspects of this revaluation in the work of Goethe and Schopenhauer and in early nineteenth-century psychology and physiology, where the very nature of sensation and perception takes on many of the features of equivalence and indifference that will later characterize photography and other networks of commodities and signs. It is this visual "nihilism" that is in the forefront of empirical studies of subjective vision, a vision that encompasses an autonomous perception severed from any external referent. What must be emphasized, however, is that this new autonomy and abstraction of vision is not only a precondition for modernist painting in the later nineteenth century but also for forms of visual mass culture appearing much earlier. In chapter 4, I discuss how optical devices that became forms of mass entertainment, such as the stereoscope and the phenakistiscope, originally derived from new empirical knowledge of the physiological status of the observer and of vision. Thus certain forms of visual experience usually uncritically categorized as "realism" are in fact bound up in *non-veridical* theories of vision that effectively annihilate a real world. Visual experience in the nineteenth century, despite all the attempts to authenticate and naturalize it, no longer has anything like the apodictic claims of the camera obscura to establish its truth. On a superficial level the fictions of realism operate undisturbed, but the processes of modernization in the nineteenth century did not depend on such illusions. New modes of circulation, communication, production, consumption, and rationalization all demanded and shaped a new kind of observer-consumer.

What I call the observer is actually just one effect of the construction of a new kind of subject or individual in the nineteenth century. The work of

Michel Foucault has been crucial for its delineation of processes and institutions that rationalized and modernized the subject, in the context of social
and economic transformations.[17] Without making causal connections, Foucault demonstrates that the industrial revolution coincided with the appearance of "new methods for administering" large populations of workers, city
dwellers, students, prisoners, hospital patients, and other groups. As individuals became increasingly torn away from older regimes of power, from agrar-
ian and artisanal production, and from large familial setups, new
decentralized arrangements were devised to control and regulate masses of
relatively free-floating subjects. For Foucault, nineteenth-century modernity
is inseparable from the way in which dispersed mechanisms of power coincide with new modes of subjectivity, and he thus details a range of pervasive
and local techniques for controlling, maintaining, and making useful new
multiplicities of individuals. Modernization consists in this production of
manageable subjects through what he calls "a certain policy of the body, a certain way of rendering a group of men docile and useful. This policy required
the involvement of definite relations of power; it called for a technique of
overlapping subjection and objectification; it brought with it new procedures
of individualization."[18]

Although he ostensibly examines "disciplinary" institutions like prisons,
schools, and the military, he also describes the role of the newly constituted
human sciences in regulating and modifying the behavior of individuals. The
management of subjects depended above all on the accumulation of knowledge about them, whether in medicine, education, psychology, physiology,
the rationalization of labor, or child care. Out of this knowledge came what
Foucault calls "a very real technology, the technology of individuals," which
he insists is "inscribed in a broad historical process: the development at about
the same time of many other technologies—agronomical, industrial,
economical."[19]

Crucial to the development of these new disciplinary techniques of the
subject was the fixing of quantitative and statistical *norms* of behavior.[20] The

17.   Michel Foucault, *Discipline and Punish,* trans. Alan Sheridan (New York, 1977).
18.   Foucault, *Discipline and Punish,* p. 305.
19.   Foucault, *Discipline and Punish,* pp. 224–225.
20.   For Georges Canguilhem, processes of normalization overlap with modernization

assessment of "normality" in medicine, psychology, and other fields became an essential part of the shaping of the individual to the requirements of institutional power in the nineteenth century, and it was through these disciplines that the subject in a sense became *visible*. My concern is how the individual as observer became an object of investigation and a locus of knowledge beginning in the first few decades of the 1800s, and how the status of the observing subject was transformed. As I have indicated, a key object of study in the empirical sciences then was subjective vision, a vision that had been taken out of the incorporeal relations of the camera obscura and relocated in the human body. It is a shift signaled by the passage from the geometrical optics of the seventeenth and eighteenth centuries to physiological optics, which dominated both scientific and philosophical discussion of vision in the nineteenth century. Thus knowledge was accumulated about the constitutive role of the body in the apprehension of a visible world, and it rapidly became obvious that efficiency and rationalization in many areas of human activity depended on information about the capacities of the human eye. One result of the new physiological optics was to expose the idiosyncrasies of the "normal" eye. Retinal afterimages, peripheral vision, binocular vision, and thresholds of attention all were studied in terms of determining quantifiable norms and parameters. The widespread preoccupation with the defects of human vision defined ever more precisely an outline of the normal, and generated new technologies for imposing a normative vision on the observer.

In the midst of such research, a number of optical devices were invented that later became elements in the mass visual culture of the nineteenth century. The phenakistiscope, one of many machines designed for the illusory simulation of movement, was produced in the midst of the empirical study of retinal afterimages; the stereoscope, a dominant form for the consumption of photographic imagery for over half a century, was first developed within the effort to quantify and formalize the physiological operation of binocular vision. What is important, then, is that these central components of nine-

---

in the nineteenth century: "Like pedagogical reform, hospital reform expresses a demand for rationalization which also appears in politics, as it appears in the economy, under the effect of nascent industrial mechanization, and which finally ends up in what has since been called normalization." *The Normal and the Pathological,* trans. Carolyn Fawcett (New York, 1989), pp. 237–238. Canguilhem asserts that the verb "to normalize" is first used in 1834.

teenth-century "realism," of mass visual culture, *preceded* the invention of photography and *in no way required* photographic procedures or even the development of mass production techniques. Rather they are inextricably dependent on a new arrangement of knowledge about the body and the constitutive relation of that knowledge to social power. These apparatuses are the outcome of a complex remaking of the individual as observer into something calculable and regularizable and of human vision into something measurable and thus exchangeable.[21] The standardization of visual imagery in the nineteenth century must be seen then not simply as part of new forms of mechanized reproduction but in relation to a broader process of normalization and subjection of the observer. If there is a revolution in the nature and function of the sign in the nineteenth century, it does not happen independently of the remaking of the subject.[22]

Readers of *Discipline and Punish* have often noted Foucault's categorical declaration, "Our society is not one of spectacle but of surveillance. . . . We are neither in the amphitheatre nor on the stage but in the Panoptic machine."[23] Although this remark occurs in the midst of a comparison between arrangements of power in antiquity and modernity, Foucault's use of the term "spectacle" is clearly bound up in the polemics of post-1968 France.

21.   Measurement takes on a primary role in a broad range of the physical sciences between 1800 and 1850, the key date being 1840 according to Thomas S. Kuhn, "The Function of Measurement in Modern Physical Science," in *The Essential Tension: Selected Studies in Scientific Tradition and Change* (Chicago, 1979), pp. 219–220. Kuhn is supported by Ian Hacking: "After 1800 or so there is an avalanche of numbers, most notably in the social sciences. . . . Perhaps a turning point was signaled in 1832, the year that Charles Babbage, inventor of the digital computer, published his brief pamphlet urging publication of tables of all the constant numbers known in the sciences and the arts." Hacking, *Representing and Intervening: Introductory Topics in the Philosophy of Natural Science* (Cambridge, 1983), pp. 234–235.
22.   Baudrillard's notion of a shift from the fixed signs of feudal and aristocratic societies to the exchangeable symbolic regime of modernity finds a reciprocal transformation articulated by Foucault in terms of the individual: "The moment that saw the transition from historico-ritual mechanisms for the formation of individuality to the scientifico-disciplinary mechanisms, when the normal took over from the ancestral, and measurement from status, thus substituting for the individuality of the memorable man that of the calculable man, that moment when the sciences of man became possible is the moment when a new technology of power and a new political anatomy of the body were implemented." *Discipline and Punish*, p. 193.
23.   Foucault, *Discipline and Punish*, p. 217.

When he wrote the book in the early 1970s, "spectacle" was an obvious allu-
sion to analyses of contemporary capitalism by Guy Debord and others.[24] One
can well imagine Foucault's disdain, as he wrote one of the greatest meditations on modernity and power, for any facile or superficial use of "spectacle"
as an explanation of how the masses are "controlled" or "duped" by media
images.[25]

But Foucault's opposition of surveillance and spectacle seems to over-
look how the effects of these two regimes of power can coincide. Using Bentham's panopticon as a primary theoretical object, Foucault relentlessly
emphasizes the ways in which human subjects became objects of observation,
in the form of institutional control or scientific and behavioral study; but he
neglects the new forms by which vision itself became a kind of discipline or
mode of work. The nineteenth-century optical devices I discuss, no less than
the panopticon, involved arrangements of bodies in space, regulations of
activity, and the deployment of individual bodies, which codified and normalized the observer within rigidly defined systems of visual consumption.
They were techniques for the management of attention, for imposing homogeneity, anti-nomadic procedures that fixed and isolated the observer using
"partitioning and cellularity . . . in which the individual is reduced as a political force." The organization of mass culture did not proceed on some other
inessential or superstructural area of social practice; it was fully embedded
within the same transformations Foucault outlines.

I am hardly suggesting, however, that the "society of the spectacle" suddenly appears alongside the developments I am detailing here. The "spectacle," as Debord uses the term, probably does not effectively take shape until
several decades into the twentieth century.[26] In this book, I am offering some

24.   Guy Debord, *The Society of the Spectacle,* trans. Donald Nicholson-Smith (New York,
1990). First published in France in 1967.
25.   On the place of vision in Foucault's thought, see Gilles Deleuze, *Foucault,* pp. 46–
69. See also John Rajchman, "Foucault's Art of Seeing," *October* 44 (Spring 1988), pp. 89–
117.
26.   Following up on a brief remark by Debord, I have discussed the case for placing the
onset of the "society of the spectacle" in the late 1920s, concurrent with the technological
and institutional origins of television, the beginning of synchronized sound in movies, the
use of mass media techniques by the Nazi party in Germany, the rise of urbanism, and the
political failure of surrealism in France, in my "Spectacle, Attention, Counter-Memory,"
October 50 (Fall 1989), pp. 97–107.

notes on its prehistory, on the early background of the spectacle. Debord, in a well-known passage, poses one of its main features:

> Since the spectacle's job is to cause a world that is no longer directly perceptible to be *seen* via different specialized media- tions, it is inevitable that it should elevate the human sense of sight to the special place once occupied by touch; the most abstract of the senses, and the most easily deceived, sight is naturally the most readily adaptable to present-day society's generalized abstraction.[27]

Thus, in my delineation of a modernization and revaluation of vision, I indi- cate how the sense of touch had been an integral part of classical theories of vision in the seventeenth and eighteenth centuries. The subsequent dissocia- tion of touch from sight occurs within a pervasive "separation of the senses" and industrial remapping of the body in the nineteenth century. The loss of touch as a conceptual component of vision meant the unloosening of the eye from the network of referentiality incarnated in tactility and its subjective rela- tion to perceived space. This autonomization of sight, occurring in many dif- ferent domains, was a historical condition for the rebuilding of an observer fitted for the tasks of "spectacular" consumption. Not only did the empirical isolation of vision allow its quantification and homogenization but it also enabled the new objects of vision (whether commodities, photographs, or the act of perception itself) to assume a mystified and abstract identity, sundered from any relation to the observer's position within a cognitively unified field. The stereoscope is one major cultural site on which this breach between tan- gibility and visuality is singularly evident.

If Foucault describes some of the epistemological and institutional con- ditions of the observer in the nineteenth century, others have detailed the actual shape and density of the field in which perception was transformed. Perhaps more than anyone else, Walter Benjamin has mapped out the het- erogeneous texture of events and objects out of which the observer in that century was composed. In the diverse fragments of his writings, we encounter

27.   Debord, *The Society of the Spectacle*, sec. 18.

an ambulatory observer shaped by a convergence of new urban spaces, technologies, and new economic and symbolic functions of images and products—forms of artificial lighting, new use of mirrors, glass and steel
architecture, railroads, museums, gardens, photography, fashion, crowds. Perception for Benjamin was acutely temporal and kinetic; he makes clear how
modernity subverts even the possibility of a contemplative beholder. There
is never a pure access to a single object; vision is always multiple, adjacent to
and overlapping with other objects, desires, and vectors. Even the congealed
space of the museum cannot transcend a world where everything is in
circulation.

It should not go unremarked that one topic is generally unexamined by
Benjamin: nineteenth-century painting. It simply is not a significant part of the
field of which he provides a rich inventory. Of the many things this omission
implies, it certainly indicates that for him painting was not a *primary* element
in the reshaping of perception in the nineteenth century.[28] The observer of
paintings in the nineteenth century was always also an observer who simultaneously consumed a proliferating range of optical and sensory experiences.
In other words, paintings were produced and assumed meaning not in some
impossible kind of aesthetic isolation, or in a continuous tradition of painterly
codes, but as one of many consumable and fleeting elements within an
expanding chaos of images, commodities, and stimulation.

One of the few visual artists that Benjamin discusses is Charles Meryon,
mediated through the sensibility of Baudelaire.[29] Meryon is important not for
the formal or iconographic content of this work, but as an index of a damaged
sensorium responding to the early shocks of modernization. Meryon's disturbing images of the mineral inertness of a medieval Paris take on the value
of "afterimages" of an annihilated set of spaces at the onset of Second Empire
urban renewal. And the nervous crosshatched incisions of his etched plates
bespeak the atrophy of artisanal handicraft in the face of serial industrial
reproduction. The example of Meryon insists that vision in the nineteenth

28.   See, for example, Benjamin, *Reflections,* trans. Edmund Jephcott (New York, 1978),
p. 151: "With the increasing scope of communications systems, the significance of painting
in imparting information is reduced."
29.   Walter Benjamin, *Charles Baudelaire: A Lyric Poet in the Era of High Capitalism,*
trans. Harry Zohn (London, 1973), pp. 86–89.

century was inseparable from transience—that is, from new temporalities, speeds, experiences of flux and obsolescence, a new density and sedimentation of the structure of visual memory. Perception within the context of modernity, for Benjamin, never disclosed the world as presence. One mode was the observer as *flâneur,* a mobile consumer of a ceaseless succession of illusory commodity-like images.[30] But the destructive dynamism of modernization was also a condition for a vision that would resist its effects, a revivifying perception of the present caught up in its own historical afterimages. Ironically, "the standardized and denatured" perception of the masses, to which Benjamin sought radical alternatives, owed much of its power in the nineteenth century to the empirical study and quantification of the retinal afterimage and its particular temporality, as I indicate in chapters 3 and 4.

Nineteenth-century painting was also slighted, for very different reasons, by the founders of modern art history, a generation or two before Benjamin. It is easy to forget that art history as an academic discipline has its origins within this same nineteenth-century milieu. Three nineteenth-century developments inseparable from the institutionalization of art historical practice are: (1) historicist and evolutionary modes of thought allowing forms to be arrayed and classified as an unfolding over time; (2) sociopolitical transformations involving the creation of leisure time and the cultural enfranchisement of more sectors of urban populations, one result of which was the public art museum; and (3) new serial modes of image reproduction, which permitted both the global circulation and juxtaposition of highly credible copies of disparate artworks. Yet if nineteenth-century modernity was in part the matrix of art history, the artworks of that modernity were excluded from art history's dominant explanatory and classifying schemes, even into the early twentieth century.

For example, two crucial traditions, one stemming from Morelli and another from the Warburg School, were fundamentally unable or unwilling to include nineteenth-century art within the scope of their investigations. This in spite of the dialectical relation of these practices to the historical moment of their own emergence: the concern of Morellian connoisseurship with

---

30.   See Susan Buck-Morss, "The Flaneur, the Sandwichman, and the Whore: The Politics of Loitering," *New German Critique* 39 (Fall, 1986), pp. 99–140.

authorship and originality occurs when new technologies and forms of exchange put in question notions of the "hand," authorship, and originality; and the quest by Warburg School scholars for symbolic forms expressive of the spiritual foundations of a unified culture coincides with a collective cultural despair at the absence or impossibility of such forms in the present. Thus these overlapping modes of art history took as their privileged objects the figurative art of antiquity and the Renaissance.

What is of interest here is the penetrating recognition, subliminal or otherwise, by the founding art historians that nineteenth-century art was fundamentally discontinuous with the art of preceding centuries. Clearly, the discontinuity they sensed is not the familiar break signified by Manet and impressionism; rather it is a question of why painters as diverse as Ingres, Overbeck, Courbet, Delaroche, Meissonier, von Köbell, Millais, Gleyre, Friedrich, Cabanel, Gerôme, and Delacroix (to name only a few) together incarnated a surface of mimetic and figural representation apparently similar to but disquietingly unlike what had preceded it. The art historian's silence, indifference, or even disdain for eclecticism and "degraded" forms implied that this period constituted a radically different visual language that could not be submitted to the same methods of analysis, that could not be made to speak in the same ways, that even could not be read.[31]

The work of subsequent generations of art historians, however, soon obscured that inaugural intuition of rupture, of difference. The nineteenth century gradually became assimilated into the mainstream of the discipline through apparently dispassionate and objective examination, similar to what had happened earlier with the art of late antiquity. But in order to domesticate that strangeness from which earlier scholars had recoiled, historians explained nineteenth-century art according to models taken from the study of older art.[32] Initially, mainly formal categories from Renaissance painting

---

31.   The hostility to most contemporary art in Burckhardt, Hildebrand, Wölfflin, Riegl, and Fiedler is recounted in Michael Podro, *The Critical Historians of Art* (New Haven, 1982), pp. 66–70.

32.   One of the first influential attempts to impose the methodology and vocabulary of earlier art history onto nineteenth-century material was Walter Friedlaender, *David to Delacroix,* trans. Robert Goldwater (Cambridge, Mass., 1952); original German edition, 1930. Friedlaender describes French painting in terms of alternating classical and baroque phases.

were transferred to nineteenth-century artists, but beginning in the 1940s notions like class content and popular imagery became surrogates for traditional iconography. By inserting nineteenth-century painting into a continuous history of art and a unified discursive apparatus of explanation, however, something of its essential difference was lost. To recover that difference one must recognize how the making, the consumption, and the effectiveness of that art is dependent on an observer—and on an organization of the visible that vastly exceeds the domain conventionally examined by art history. The isolation of painting after 1830 as a viable and self-sufficient category for study becomes highly problematic, to say the least. The circulation and reception of *all* visual imagery is so closely interrelated by the middle of the century that any single medium or form of visual representation no longer has a significant autonomous identity. The meanings and effects of any single image are always adjacent to this overloaded and plural sensory environment and to the observer who inhabited it. Benjamin, for example, saw the art museum in the mid-nineteenth century as simply one of many dream spaces, experienced and traversed by an observer no differently from arcades, botanical gardens, wax museums, casinos, railway stations, and department stores.[33]

Nietzsche describes the position of the individual within this milieu in terms of a crisis of assimilation:

> Sensibility immensely more irritable; . . . the abundance of disparate impressions greater than ever: cosmopolitanism in foods, literatures, newspapers, forms, tastes, even landscapes. The tempo of this influx *prestissimo;* the impressions erase each other; one instinctively resists taking in anything, taking anything deeply, to "digest" anything; a weakening of the power to digest results from this. A kind of adaptation to the flood of impressions takes place: men unlearn spontaneous action, they merely react to stimuli from the outside.[34]

Like Benjamin, Nietzsche here undermines any possibility of a contemplative beholder and poses an anti-aesthetic distraction as a central feature of mod-

---

33.   See Walter Benjamin, *Das Passagen-Werk,* vol. 1 (Frankfurt, 1982), pp. 510–523.
34.   Friedrich Nietzsche, *The Will to Power,* trans. Walter Kaufmann and R. J. Hollingdale (New York, 1967), p. 47.

ernity, one that Georg Simmel and others were to examine in detail. When Nietzsche uses quasi-scientific words like "influx," "adaptation," "react," and "irritability," it is about a world that has already been reconfigured into new perceptual components. Modernity, in this case, coincides with the collapse of classical models of vision and their stable space of representations. Instead, observation is increasingly a question of equivalent sensations and stimuli that have no reference to a spatial location. What begins in the 1820s and 1830s is a repositioning of the observer, outside of the fixed relations of interior/exterior presupposed by the camera obscura and into an undemarcated terrain on which the distinction between internal sensation and external signs is irrevocably blurred. If there is ever a "liberation" of vision in the nineteenth century, this is when it first happens. In the absence of the juridical model of the camera obscura, there is a freeing up of vision, a falling away of the rigid structures that had shaped it and constituted its objects.

But almost simultaneous with this final dissolution of a transcendent foundation for vision emerges a plurality of means to recode the activity of the eye, to regiment it, to heighten its productivity and to prevent its distraction. Thus the imperatives of capitalist modernization, while demolishing the field of classical vision, generated techniques for imposing visual attentiveness, rationalizing sensation, and managing perception. They were disciplinary techniques that required a notion of visual experience as instrumental, modifiable, and essentially abstract, and that never allowed a real world to acquire solidity or permanence. Once vision became located in the empirical immediacy of the observer's body, it belonged to time, to flux, to death. The guarantees of authority, identity, and universality supplied by the camera obscura are of another epoch.

2   The Camera Obscura and Its Subject

This kind of knowledge seems to be the truest, the most authentic, for it has the object before itself in its entirety and completeness. This bare fact of certainty, however, is really and admittedly the abstractest and the poorest kind of truth.

—G. W. F. Hegel

A prevalent tendency in methodological discussion is to approach problems of knowledge sub specie aeternitatis, *as it were. Statements are compared with each other without regard to their history and without considering that they might belong to different historical strata.*

—Paul Feyerabend

Most attempts to theorize vision and visuality are wedded to models that emphasize a continuous and overarching Western visual tradition. Clearly it is often strategically necessary to map the outlines of a dominant Western speculative or scopic tradition of vision in some sense continuous, for instance, from Plato to the present, or from the quattrocento into the late nineteenth century. My concern is not so much to argue against these models, which have their usefulness, but rather to insist that there are some important discontinuities such monolithic constructions have obscured. Again, the specific account that interests me here, one that has become almost ubiquitous and continues to be developed in a variety of forms, is that the emergence of photography and cinema in the nineteenth century is the fulfillment of a long unfolding of technological and/or ideological development in the West whereby the camera obscura evolves into the photographic camera. Such a schema implies that at each step in this evolution the same essential presuppositions about an observer's relation to the world are in place. One could name several dozen books on the history of film or photography in whose first chapter appears the obligatory seventeenth-century engraving depicting a camera obscura, as a kind of inaugural or incipient form on a long evolutionary ladder.

These models of continuity have been used by historians of divergent and even antithetical political positions. Conservatives tend to pose an account of ever-increasing progress toward verisimilitude in representation, in which Renaissance perspective and photography are part of the same quest for a fully objective equivalent of a "natural vision." In these histories of science or culture, the camera obscura is made part of the development of the sciences of observation in Europe during the seventeenth and eighteenth centuries. The accumulation of knowledge about light, lenses, and the eye becomes part of a progressive sequence of discoveries and achievements that lead to increasingly accurate investigation and representation of the physical world. Privileged events in such a sequence usually also include the invention of linear perspective in the fifteenth century, the career of Galileo, the inductive work of Newton, and the emergence of British empiricism.

Radical historians, however, usually see the camera obscura and cinema as bound up in a single enduring apparatus of political and social power, elaborated over several centuries, that continues to discipline and regulate the status of an observer. The camera is thus seen by some as an exemplary indication of the ideological nature of representation, embodying the epistemological presumptions of "bourgeois humanism." It is often argued that the cinematic apparatus, emerging in the late nineteenth and early twentieth centuries, perpetuates, albeit in increasingly differentiated forms, the same ideology of representation and the same transcendental subject.

What I hope to do in this chapter is briefly to articulate the camera obscura model of vision in terms of its historical specificity, in order subsequently to suggest how this model collapsed in the 1820s and 1830s, when it was displaced by radically different notions of what an observer was, and of what constituted vision. If, later in the nineteenth century, cinema or photography seem to invite formal comparisons with the camera obscura, it is within a social, cultural, and scientific milieu where there had already been a profound break with the conditions of vision presupposed by this device.

It has been known for at least two thousand years that when light passes through a small hole into a dark, enclosed interior, an inverted image will appear on the wall opposite the hole. Thinkers as remote from each other as Euclid, Aristotle, Alhazen, Roger Bacon, Leonardo, and Kepler noted this phenomenon and speculated in various ways how it might or might not be analogous to the functioning of human vision. The long history of such observations has yet to be written and is far removed from the aims and limited scope of this chapter.

It is important, however, to make a distinction between the enduring empirical fact that an image can be produced in this way and the camera obscura as a historically constructed artifact. For the camera obscura was not simply an inert and neutral piece of equipment or a set of technical premises to be tinkered with and improved over the years; rather, it was embedded in a much larger and denser organization of knowledge and of the observing subject. Historically speaking, we must recognize how for nearly two hundred years, from the late 1500s to the end of the 1700s, the structural and optical principles of the camera obscura coalesced into a dominant paradigm through which was described the status and possibilities of an observer. I emphasize that this paradigm was dominant though obviously not exclusive. During the seventeenth and eighteenth centuries the camera obscura was without question the most widely used model for explaining human vision, and for representing the relation of a perceiver and the position of a knowing subject to an external world. This highly problematic object was far more than

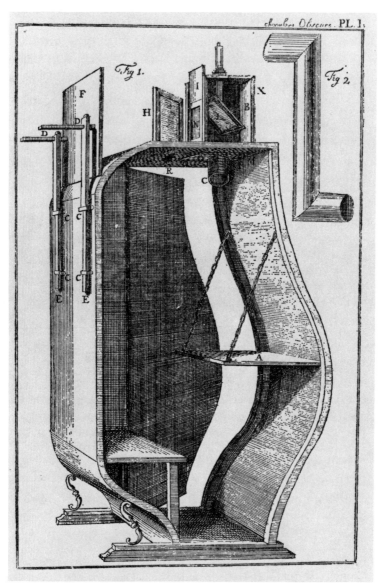

Portable camera obscura. Mid-eighteenth century.

simply an optical device. For over two hundred years it subsisted as a philo-sophical metaphor, a model in the science of physical optics, *and* was also a technical apparatus used in a large range of cultural activities.[1] For two cen-turies it stood as model, in both rationalist and empiricist thought, of how observation leads to truthful inferences about the world; at the same time the physical incarnation of that model was a widely used means of observing the visible world, an instrument of popular entertainment, of scientific inquiry, and of artistic practice. The formal operation of a camera obscura as an abstract diagram may remain constant, but the function of the device or met-aphor within an actual social or discursive field has fluctuated decisively. The fate of the camera obscura paradigm in the nineteenth century is a case in point.[2] In the texts of Marx, Bergson, Freud, and others the very apparatus that a century earlier was the site of truth becomes a model for procedures and forces that conceal, invert, and mystify truth.[3]

1.   The extensive literature on the camera obscura is summarized in Aaron Scharf, *Art and Photography* (Harmondsworth, 1974), and in Lawrence Gowing, *Vermeer* (New York, 1952). General studies not mentioned in those works are Moritz von Rohr, *Zur Entwick-lung der dunkeln Kammer* (Berlin, 1925), and John J. Hammond, *The Camera Obscura: A Chronicle* (Bristol, 1981). For valuable information on the uses of the camera obscura in the eighteenth century, see Helmuth Fritzsche, *Bernardo Belotto genannt Canaletto* (Magdeburg, 1936) pp. 158–194, and Decio Gioseffi, *Canaletto; Il quaderno delle Gallerie Veneziane e l'impiego della camera ottica* (Trieste, 1959). Works on the artistic use of the camera obscura in the seventeenth century include Charles Seymour, Jr., "Dark Chamber and Light-Filled room: Vermeer and the Camera Obscura," *Art Bulletin* 46, no. 3 (Septem-ber 1964), pp. 323–331; Daniel A. Fink, "Vermeer's Use of the Camera Obscura: A Com-parative Study," *Art Bulletin* 53, no. 4 (December 1971), pp. 493–505; A. Hyatt Mayor, "The Photographic Eye," *Metropolitan Museum of Art Bulletin* 5, no. 1 (Summer 1946), pp. 15–26; Heinrich Schwarz, "Vermeer and the Camera Obscura," *Pantheon* 24 (May –June 1966), pp. 170–180; Arthur K. Wheelock, *Perspective, Optics, and Delft Artists Around 1650* (New York, 1977); and Joel Snyder, "Picturing Vision," *Critical Inquiry* 6 (Spring 1980), pp. 499–526.
2.   Cf. Colin Murray Turbayne, *The Myth of Metaphor* (New Haven, 1962), esp. pp. 154–158, 203–208, which poses the camera obscura as a completely ahistorical concept linked with representative or copy theories of perception from antiquity to the present. An equally ahistorical discussion of the structure of modern photography and of the Cartesian camera obscura is Arthur Danto, "The Representational Character of Ideas and the Problem of the External World," in *Descartes: Critical and Interpretative Essays,* ed. Michael Hooker (Bal-timore, 1978), pp. 287–298.
3.   Karl Marx, *The German Ideology,* ed. C. J. Arthur (New York, 1970), p. 47; Henri Berg-son, *Matter and Memory* [1896] trans. N. M. Paul and W. S. Palmer (New York, 1988), pp. 37–39; Sigmund Freud, *The Interpretation of Dreams,* trans. James Strachey (New York,

What then allows me to suggest that there is a common coherence to the status of the camera obscura in the seventeenth and eighteenth centuries, to pose this broad expanse of time as a unity? Clearly the physical and operational makeup of the camera obscura underwent continual modification during this period.[4] For example, the first portable devices were in use by 1650, and into the late 1700s models became increasingly small. And obviously the wide range of social and representational practices associated with the instrument mutated considerably over two centuries. Yet despite the multiplicity of its local manifestations, what is extraordinary is the consistency with which certain primary features of the camera obscura are repeated throughout this period. There is a *regularity* and uniformity with which the formal relations constituted by the camera are *stated* again and again, no matter how heterogeneous or unrelated the locations of those statements.

I am hardly suggesting, however, that the camera obscura had simply a discursive identity. If we can designate it in terms of statements, every one of those statements is necessarily linked to subjects, practices, and institutions. Perhaps the most important obstacle to an understanding of the camera obscura, or of any optical apparatus, is the idea that optical device and observer are two distinct entities, that the identity of observer exists independently from the optical device that is a physical piece of technical equipment. For what constitutes the camera obscura is precisely its multiple identity, its "mixed" status as an epistemological figure within a discursive order *and* an object within an arrangement of cultural practices.[5] The camera obscura is what Gilles Deleuze would call an *assemblage,* something that is

---

1955), pp. 574–575. Hegel's notion of "the inverted world" (*verkehrte Welt*) is crucial for subsequent repudiations of the camera obscura model; see *Phenomenology of Mind,* trans. J. B. Baillie (New York, 1967), pp. 203–207. See also Sarah Kofman, *Camera obscura de l'idéologie* (Paris, 1973); Constance Penley, Janet Bergstrom et al., "Critical Approaches," *Camera Obscura* no. 1 (Fall 1976), pp. 3–10; and W. J. T. Mitchell, *Iconology: Image, Text, Ideology* (Chicago, 1986), pp. 160–208.

4.   For details on various models during this period, see, for example, Gioseffi, *Canaletto,* pp. 13–22.

5.   "The distinctions with which the materialist method, discriminative from the outset, starts are distinctions within this highly mixed object, and it cannot present this object as mixed or uncritical enough." Walter Benjamin, *Charles Baudelaire: A Lyric Poet in the Era of High Capitalism,* trans. Harry Zohn (London, 1973), p. 103.

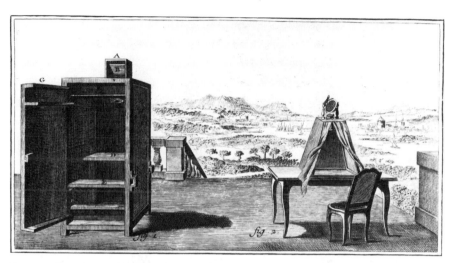

Camera obscuras. Mid-eighteenth century.

"simultaneously and inseparably a machinic assemblage and an assemblage
of enunciation," an object about which something is said and at the same time
an object that is used.[6] It is a site at which a discursive formation intersects with
material practices. The camera obscura, then, cannot be reduced either to a
technological or a discursive object: it was a complex social amalgam in which
its existence as a textual figure was never separable from its machinic uses.

What this implies is that the camera obscura must be extricated from the
evolutionary logic of a technological determinism, central to influential historical surveys, which position it as a precursor or an inaugural event in a
genealogy leading to the birth of photography.[7] To cite Deleuze again,
"Machines are social before being technical."[8] Obviously photography had

6.   Gilles Deleuze and Félix Guattari, *A Thousand Plateaus: Capitalism and Schizophrenia,* trans. Brian Massumi (Minneapolis, 1987), p. 504.
7.   Overwhelmingly, the starting point of histories of photography is the camera
obscura as a photographic camera in embryo. The birth of photography is then "explained"
as the fortuitous encounter of this optical device with new discoveries in photochemistry.
See, for example, Helmut Gernsheim, *A Concise History of Photography* (New York, 1965),
pp. 9–15; Beaumont Newhall, *The History of Photography* (New York, 1964), pp. 11–13;
Josef Maria Eder, *History of Photography,* trans. Edward Epstein (New York, 1945) pp. 36–
52; and Heinrich Schwarz, *Art and Photography: Forerunners and Influences* (Chicago,
1985), pp. 97–117.
8.   Gilles Deleuze, *Foucault,* trans. Seán Hand (Minneapolis, 1988), p. 13.

technical and material underpinnings, and the structural principles of the two devices are clearly not unrelated. I will argue, however, that the camera obscura and the photographic camera, as assemblages, practices, and social objects, belong to two fundamentally different organizations of representation and the observer, as well as of the observer's relation to the visible. By the beginning of the nineteenth century the camera obscura is no longer synonymous with the production of truth and with an observer positioned to see truthfully. The regularity of such statements ends abruptly; the assemblage constituted by the camera breaks down and the photographic camera becomes an essentially dissimilar object, lodged amidst a radically different network of statements and practices.

Art historians, predictably, tend to be interested in art objects, and most of them have thus considered the camera obscura for how it may have determined the formal structure of paintings or prints. Many accounts of the camera obscura, particularly those dealing with the eighteenth century, tend to consider it exclusively in terms of its use by artists for copying, and as an aid in the making of paintings. There is often a presumption that artists were making do with an inadequate substitute for what they really wanted, and which would soon appear—that is, a photographic camera.[9] Such an emphasis imposes a set of twentieth-century assumptions, in particular a productivist logic, onto a device whose primary function was *not* to generate pictures. Copying with the camera obscura—that is, the tracing and making permanent of its image—was only one of its many uses, and even by the mid-eighteenth century was de-emphasized in a number of important accounts. The article on "camera obscura" in the *Encyclopédie,* for example, lists its uses in this order:

9.   Arthur K. Wheelock proposes that the "verisimilitude" of the camera obscura satisfied the naturalistic urges of seventeenth-century Dutch painters who found perspective too mechanical and abstract. "For Dutch artists, intent on exploring the world about them, the camera obscura offered a unique means for judging what a truly natural painting should look like." "Constantijn Huygens and Early Attitudes Towards the Camera Obscura," *History of Photography* 1, no. 2 (April 1977), pp. 93–101. As well as proposing the highly questionable notion of a "truly natural" painting, Wheelock assumes that the device allowed a neutral, unproblematic presentation of visual "reality." He outlines a process of stylistic change, apparently following Gombrich, in which the use of the camera obscura interacted with traditional practices and schemas to yield more lifelike images. See *Perspective, Optics, and Delft Artists,* pp. 165–184. Svetlana Alpers, *The Art of Describing* (Chicago, 1983), pp. 32–33, also asserts that the camera obscura implied a more truthful image.

"It throws great light on the nature of vision; it provides a very diverting spectacle, in that it presents images perfectly resembling their objects; it represents the colors and movements of objects better than any other sort of representation is able to do." Only belatedly does it note that "by means of this instrument someone who does not know how to draw is able nevertheless to draw with extreme accuracy."[10] Noninstrumental descriptions of the camera obscura are pervasive, emphasizing it as a self-sufficient demonstration of its own activity and by analogy of human vision. For those who understood its optical underpinnings it offered the spectacle of representation operating completely transparently, and for those ignorant of its principles it afforded the pleasures of illusion. Just as perspective contained within it the disruptive possibilities of anamorphoses, however, so the veracity of the camera was haunted by its proximity to techniques of conjuration and illusion. The magic lantern that developed alongside the camera obscura had the capacity to appropriate the setup of the latter and subvert its operation by infusing its interior with reflected and projected images using artificial light.[11] However, this counter-deployment of the camera obscura never occupied an effective discursive or social position from which to challenge the dominant model I have been outlining here.

10. *Encyclopédie ou dictionnaire des sciences, des arts et des métiers,* vol. 3 (Paris, 1753), pp. 62–64. Earlier in the century John Harris does not mention its use by artists or the possibility of recording the projected images. Instead he emphasizes its status as a popular entertainment and a didactic illustration of the principles of vision. See his *Lexicon Technicum: or a Universal English Dictionary of Arts and Sciences* (London, 1704), pp. 264–273. William Molyneux is also silent about any artistic use of the device but closely associates it with the magic lantern and peep-shows in his *Dioptrica nova: A Treatise of dioptricks in two parts* (London, 1692), pp. 36–41. For a typical handbook on artists' use of the camera obscura see Charles-Antoine Jombert, *Méthode pour apprendre le dessein* (Paris, 1755), pp. 137–156.

11. The work of the Jesuit priest Athanasius Kircher (1602–1680) and his legendary magic-lantern technology is a crucial counter-use of classical optical systems. See his *Ars magna lucis et umbrae* (Rome, 1646), pp. 173–184. In place of the transparent access of observer to exterior, Kircher devised techniques for flooding the inside of the camera with a visionary brilliance, using various artificial light sources, mirrors, projected images, and sometimes translucent gems in place of a lens to simulate divine illumination. In contrast to the Counter-Reformation background of Kircher's practices, it's possible to make a very general association of the camera obscura with the inwardness of a modernized and Protestant subjectivity.

At the same time one must be wary of conflating the meanings and effects of the camera obscura with techniques of linear perspective. Obviously the two are related, but it must be stressed that the camera obscura defines the position of an interiorized observer to an exterior world, not just to a two-dimensional representation, as is the case with perspective. Thus the camera obscura is synonymous with a much broader kind of subject-effect; it is about far more than the relation of an observer to a certain procedure of picture making. Many contemporary accounts of the camera obscura single out as its most impressive feature its representation of movement. Observers frequently spoke with astonishment of the flickering images within the camera of pedestrians in motion or branches moving in the wind as being more life-like than the original objects.[12] Thus the phenomenological differences between the experience of a pespectival construction and the projection of the camera obscura are not even comparable. What is crucial about the camera obscura is its relation of the observer to the undemarcated, undifferentiated expanse of the world outside, and how its apparatus makes an orderly cut or delimitation of that field allowing it to be viewed, without sacrificing the vitality of its being. But the movement and temporality so evident in the camera obscura were always prior to the act of representation; movement and time could be seen and experienced, but never represented.[13]

Another key misconception about the camera obscura is that it is somehow intrinsically a "Northern" model of visuality.[14] Svetlana Alpers, in particular, has developed this position in her insistence that the essential

12.   See, for example, Robert Smith, *Compleat System of Opticks* (Cambridge, 1738), p. 384, and John Harris, *Lexicon Technicum,* p. 40.

13.   Classical science in the seventeenth and eighteenth centuries extracted "individual realities from the complex continuum which nourished them and gave them shape, made them manageable, even intelligible, but always transformed them in essence. Cut off from those precarious aspects of phenomena that can only be called their "becoming," that is, their aleatory and transformative adventure *in time* including their often extreme sensitivity to secondary, tertiary, stochastic, or merely invisible processes, and cut off as well from their effective capacities to affect or determine in their turn effects at the heart of these same processes—the science of nature has excluded time and rendered itself incapable of thinking change or novelty in and for itself." Sanford Kwinter, *Immanence and Event* (forthcoming).

14.   Much speculation about the history of the camera obscura assumes its origins are Mediterranean—that it was accidentally "discovered" when bright sunlight would enter through a small aperture in shuttered windows.

characteristics of seventeenth-century Dutch painting are inseparable from the experience in the North of the camera obscura.[15] Missing, however, from her discussion is a sense of how the metaphor of the camera obscura as a figure for human vision pervaded all of Europe during the seventeenth century. She refers to her "Northern descriptive mode" as the "Keplerian mode," based on Kepler's important statements about the camera obscura and the retinal image. But Kepler (whose optical studies were done in the eclectic and hardly Northern visual culture of the Prague court of Rudolf II) was merely one of a number of major seventeenth-century thinkers in whose work the camera obscura holds a central position, including Leibniz, Descartes, Newton, and Locke.[16] Over and above the question of the meanings of Dutch art, it is important to acknowledge the *transnational* character of intellectual and scientific life in Europe during this period, and more specifically the fundamental similarities linking accounts of the camera obscura, whether by rationalists or empiricists, from diverse parts of Europe.[17]

Although she addresses a traditional art historical problem (the style of Northern versus Italian painting), in the course of her argument Alpers makes some broad speculations about the historical role of the camera obscura. While her argument cannot be fully summarized here, she outlines a "descriptive" and empirical mode of seeing, coincident with the experience of the

15.   Svetlana Alpers, *The Art of Describing: Dutch Art in the Seventeenth Century* (Chicago, 1983), pp. 27–33.

16.   Alpers's omission of Descartes's account of vision and the camera obscura in *La dioptrique* (1637) is notable, given that Descartes lived in Holland for over twenty years, from 1628 to 1649, and that his optical theory was so closely related to Kepler's. The similarity of a Keplerian and a Cartesian observer tends to undermine the notion of distinct regional epistemes. On Descartes and Holland see, for example, C. Louise Thijssen, "Le cartésianisme aux Pays-Bas," in E. J. Dijksterhuis, ed., *Descartes et le cartésianisme hollandais: Etudes et documents* (Paris, 1950), pp. 183–260. Gérard Simon insists that Descartes's *La dioptrique* "only confirmed and made more precise" all the important features of Kepler's optics, including the theory of the retinal image, in "A propos de la théorie de la perception visuelle chez Kepler et Descartes," in *Proceedings of XIIIth International Congress of the History of Science,* vol. 6 (Moscow, 1974), pp. 237–245.

17.   In a related problem, Erwin Panofsky noted the different uses of perspective in the North and the South, but he leaves no doubt that what these uses have in common as system and technique is far more important than regional idiosyncracies. See "Die Perspektive als 'Symbolische Form,'" in *Vorträge der Bibliothek Warburg* (1924–25), pp. 258–330. (English trans. by Christopher S. Wood forthcoming from Zone Books, New York.)

camera obscura, as a permanent "artistic option" in Western art. "It is an option or pictorial mode that has been taken up at different times for different reasons and it remains unclear to what extent it should be considered to constitute, in and of itself, a historical development."[18] She asserts that "the ultimate origins of photography do not lie in the fifteenth-century invention of perspective, but rather in the alternative mode of the North. Seen this way, one might say that the photographic image, the Dutch art of describing, and . . . Impressionist painting are all examples of this constant artistic option in the art of the West."[19] My aim, on the contrary, is to suggest that what *separates* photography from both perspective and the camera obscura is far more significant than what they have in common.

While my discussion of the camera obscura is founded on notions of *discontinuity* and *difference,* Alpers, like many others, poses notions of both *continuity* in her lineage of the origins of photography and *identity* in her idea of an a priori observer who has perpetual access to these free-floating and transhistorical options of seeing.[20] If these options are "constant," the observer in question becomes removed from the specific material and historical conditions of vision. Such an argument, in its reclothing of familiar stylistic polarities, runs the risk of becoming a kind of neo-Wölfflinism.

Standard accounts of the camera obscura routinely give some special mention of the Neapolitan savant Giovanni Battista della Porta, often identified as one of its inventors.[21] Such details we will never know for sure, but we do have his description of a camera obscura in the widely read *Magia Naturalis* of 1558, in which he explains the use of a concave speculum to insure that the projected image will not be inverted. In the second edition of 1589, della Porta details how a concave lens can be placed in the aperture of the camera to produce a much more finely resolved image. But della Porta's significance concerns the intellectual threshold that he straddles, and how his camera obscura

18.   Svetlana Alpers, *The Art of Describing,* p. 244, n37.
19.   Alpers, *The Art of Describing,* p. 244, n37.
20.   For an important discussion of identity and difference in historical explanation, see Fredric Jameson, "Marxism and Historicism," in *The Ideologies of Theory: Essays 1971–1986,* vol. 2 (Minneapolis, 1988), pp. 148–177.
21.   See Mario Gliozzi, "L'invenzione della camera oscura," *Archivio di Storia Della Scienza* xiv (April-June 1932), pp. 221–229.

inaugurates an organization of knowledge and seeing that will undermine the Renaissance science that most of his work exemplifies.[22]

The natural magic of della Porta was a conception of the world in its fundamental unity *and* a means of observing this unity: "We are persuaded that the knowledge of secret things depends upon the contemplation and the view of the whole world, namely the motion, style and fashion thereof."[23] Elsewhere della Porta insists that "one must watch the phenomena with the eyes of a lynx so that, when observation is complete, one can begin to manipulate them."[24] The observer here is ultimately seeking insight into a universal language of symbols and analogies that might be employed in the directing and harnessing of the forces of nature. But according to Michel Foucault, della Porta envisioned a world in which all things were adjacent to each other, linked together in a chain:

> In the vast syntax of the world, the different beings adjust themselves to one another, the plant communicates with the animal, the earth with the sea, man with everything around him. . . . The relation of emulation enables things to imitate one another from one end of the universe to the other . . . by duplicating itself in a mirror the world abolishes the distance proper to it; in this way it overcomes the place allotted to each thing. But which of these images coursing through space are the original images? Which is the reality and which is the projection?[25]

This interlacing of nature and its representation, this indistinction between reality and its projection will be abolished by the camera obscura, and instead it will institute an optical regime that will a priori separate and distinguish image from object.[26] In fact della Porta's account of the camera obscura was

22.   Della Porta is identified as a "pre-modern" in Robert Lenoble, *Histoire de l'idée de nature* (Paris, 1969), p. 27.

23.   Giovanni Battista della Porta, *Natural Magick* (London, 1658), p. 15.

24.   Cited in Eugenio Garin, *Italian Humanism: Philosophy and Civic Life in the Renaissance,* trans. Peter Munz (New York, 1965), p. 190.

25.   Michel Foucault, *The Order of Things,* pp. 18–19.

26.   We should note della Porta's indifference to the real or illusory status of what the camera obscura makes visible: "Nothing can be more pleasant for great men and Scholars, and ingenious persons to behold; That in a dark Chamber by white sheets objected, one may see as clearly and perspicuously, as if they were before his eyes, Huntings, Banquets,

a key element in Kepler's theoretical formulation of the retinal image.[27] Ernst Cassirer places della Porta within the Renaissance tradition of magic, in which to contemplate an object

> means to become one with it. But this unity is only possible if the subject and the object, the knower and the known, are of the same nature; they must be members and parts of one and the same vital complex. Every sensory perception is an act of fusion and reunification.[28]

For della Porta's natural magic, the use of the camera obscura was simply one of a number of methods that allowed an observer to become more fully concentrated on a particular object; it had no exclusive priority as the site or mode of observation. But to readers of della Porta several decades later, the camera obscura seemed to promise an unrivaled and privileged means of observation that was attained finally at the cost of shattering the Renaissance adjacency of knower and known.

Beginning in the late 1500s the figure of the camera obscura begins to assume a preeminent importance in delimiting and defining the relations between observer and world. Within several decades the camera obscura is no longer one of many instruments or visual options but instead the compulsory site from which vision can be conceived or represented. Above all it indicates the appearance of a new model of subjectivity, the hegemony of a new subject-effect. First of all the camera obscura performs an operation of

---

Armies of Enemies, Plays and all things else that one desireth. Let there be over against that Chamber, where you desire to represent these things, some spacious Plain, where the sun can freely shine: upon that you shall set trees in Order, also Woods, Mountains, Rivers and Animals that are really so, or made by Art, of Wood, or some other matter . . . those that are in the Chamber shall see Trees, Animals, Hunters, Faces, and all the rest so plainly, that they cannot tell whether they be true or delusions: Swords drawn will glister in at the hole." Giovanni Battista della Porta, *Natural Magick,* pp. 364–365.

27.   For the influence of della Porta on Kepler, see David C. Lindberg, *Theories of Vision from Al-Kindi to Kepler* (Chicago, 1976), pp. 182–206.

28.   Ernst Cassirer, *The Individual and the Cosmos in Renaissance Philosophy,* trans. Mario Domandi (Philadelphia, 1972), p. 148. For more on della Porta, see Miller H. Rienstra, *Giovanni Battista della Porta and Renaissance Science* (Ph.D. diss., University of Michigan, 1963).

Camera obscura. 1646.

individuation; that is, it necessarily defines an observer as isolated, enclosed, and autonomous within its dark confines. It impels a kind of *askesis,* or withdrawal from the world, in order to regulate and purify one's relation to the manifold contents of the now "exterior" world. Thus the camera obscura is inseparable from a certain metaphysic of interiority: it is a figure for both the observer who is nominally a free sovereign individual and a privatized subject confined in a quasi-domestic space, cut off from a public exterior world.[29] (Jacques Lacan has noted that Bishop Berkeley and others wrote about visual representations as if they were private property.)[30] At the same time, another related and equally decisive function of the camera was to sunder the act of seeing from the physical body of the observer, to decorporealize vision. The monadic viewpoint of the individual is authenticated and legitimized by the camera obscura, but the observer's physical and sensory experience is supplanted by the relations between a mechanical apparatus and a pre-given

29.   Georg Lukács describes this type of artificially isolated individual in *History and Class Consciousness,* pp. 135–138. See also the excellent discussion of inwardness and sexual privatization in the seventeenth century in Francis Barker, *The Tremulous Private Body: Essays on Subjection* (London, 1984), pp. 9–69.

30.   Jacques Lacan, *The Four Fundamental Concepts of Psycho-Analysis,* trans. Alan Sheridan (New York, 1978), p. 81.

world of objective truth. Nietzsche summarizes this kind of thought: "The senses deceive, reason corrects the errors; consequently, one concluded, reason is the road to the constant; the least sensual ideas must be closest to the 'true world.'—It is from the senses that most misfortunes come—they are deceivers, deluders, destroyers."[31]

Among the well-known texts in which we find the image of the camera obscura and of its interiorized and disembodied subject are Newton's *Opticks* (1704) and Locke's *Essay on Human Understanding* (1690). What they jointly demonstrate is how the camera obscura was a model simultaneously for the observation of empirical phenomena *and* for reflective introspection and self-observation. The site of Newton's inductive procedures throughout his text is the camera obscura; it is the ground on which his knowledge is made possible. Near the beginning of the *Opticks* he recounts:

> In a very dark Chamber, at a round hole, about one third Part of an Inch, broad, made in the shut of a window, I placed a glass prism, whereby the Beam of the Sun's Light, which came in at that Hole, might be refracted upwards toward the opposite wall of the chamber, and there form a coloured image of the Sun.[32]

The physical activity that Newton describes with the first person pronoun refers not to the operation of his own vision but rather to his deployment of a transparent, refractive means of representation. Newton is less the observer than he is the organizer, the stager of an apparatus from whose actual functioning he is physically distinct. Although the apparatus in question is not strictly a camera obscura (a prism is substituted for a plane lens or pinhole), its structure is fundamentally the same: the representation of an exterior phenomenon occurs within the rectilinear confines of a darkened room, a chamber, or, in Locke's words, an "empty cabinet."[33] The two-dimensional plane on which the image of an exterior presents itself subsists only in its specific rela-

31.   Friedrich Nietzsche, *The Will to Power*, p. 317.
32.   Sir Isaac Newton, *Opticks, or a Treatise of the Reflections, Refractions, Inflections and Colours of Light*, 4th ed. (1730; rpt. New York, 1952), p. 26.
33.   John Locke, *An Essay Concerning Human Understanding*, ed. Alexander Campbell Fraser (New York, 1959), I,ii, 15. On some of the epistemological implications of Newton's work, see Stephen Toulmin, "The Inwardness of Mental Life," *Critical Inquiry* (Autumn 1979), pp. 1–16.

tion of distance to an aperture in the wall opposite it. But between these two locations (a point and a plane) is an indeterminate extensive space in which an observer is ambiguously situated. Unlike a perspectival construction, which also presumed to represent an objectively ordered representation, the camera obscura did not dictate a restricted site or area from which the image presents its full coherence and consistency.[34] On one hand the observer is disjunct from the pure operation of the device and is there as a disembodied witness to a mechanical and transcendental re-presentation of the objectivity of the world. On the other hand, however, his or her presence in the camera implies a spatial and temporal simultaneity of human subjectivity and objective apparatus. Thus the spectator is a more free-floating inhabitant of the darkness, a marginal supplementary presence independent of the machinery of representation. As Foucault demonstrated in his analysis of Velasquez's *Las Meninas,* it is a question of a subject incapable of self-representation as both subject and object.[35] The camera obscura *a priori* prevents the observer from seeing his or her position as part of the representation. The body then is a problem the camera could never solve except by marginalizing it into a phantom in order to establish a space of reason.[36] In a sense, the camera obscura is a precarious figurative resolution of what Edmund Husserl defined as the major philosophical problem of the seventeenth century: "How a philosophizing which seeks its ultimate foundations in the subjective . . . can claim an objectively 'true' and metaphysically transcendent validity."[37]

Perhaps the most famous image of the camera obscura is in Locke's *Essay Concerning Human Understanding* (1690):

> External and internal sensations are the only passages that I can
> find of knowledge to the understanding. These alone, as far as I can

34.   Hubert Damisch has stressed that late quattrocento perspectival constructions allowed a viewer a limited field of mobility from within which the consistency of the painting was maintained, rather than from the immobility of a fixed and single point. See his *L'origine de la perspective* (Paris, 1988). See also Jacques Aumont, "Le point de vue," *Communications* 38, 1983, pp. 3–29.

35.   Foucault, *The Order of Things,* pp. 3–16. See also Hubert Dreyfus and Paul Rabinow, *Michel Foucault: Beyond Structuralism and Hermeneutics* (Chicago, 1982), p. 25.

36.   On Galileo, Descartes, and "the occultation of the enunciating subject in discursive activity," see Timothy J. Reiss, *The Discourse of Modernism* (Ithaca, 1982), pp. 38–43.

37.   Edmund Husserl, *The Crisis of European Science and Transcendental Phenomenology,* trans. David Carr (Evanston, Ill., 1970), p. 81.

discover, are the windows by which light is let into this *dark room*. For, methinks, the understanding is not much unlike a closet wholly shut from light, with only some little opening left . . . to let in external visible resemblances, or some idea of things without; would the pictures coming into such a dark room but stay there and lie so orderly as to be found upon occasion it would very much resemble the understanding of a man.[38]

An important feature of Locke's text here is how the metaphor of the dark room effectively distances us from the apparatus he describes. As part of his general project of introspection Locke proposes a means of visualizing spatially the operations of the intellect. He makes explicit what was implied in Newton's account of his activity in his dark chamber: the eye of the observer is completely separate from the apparatus that allows the entrance and formation of "pictures" or "resemblances." Hume also insisted on a similar relation of distance: "The operations of the mind . . . must be apprehended in an instant by a *superior* penetration, derived from nature and improved by habit and reflection."[39]

Elsewhere in Locke's text another meaning is given to the idea of the room, of what it literally meant in seventeenth-century England to be *in camera,* that is, within the chambers of a judge or person of title. Locke writes that sensations are conveyed "from without to their audience in the brain—the mind's presence room, as I may so call it."[40] In addition to structuring the act of observation as the process by which something is observed by a subject, Locke also gives a new juridical role to the observer within the camera obscura. Thus he modifies the receptive and neutral function of the apparatus by specifying a more self-legislative and authoritative function: the camera obscura allows the subject to guarantee and police the correspondence

38.   Locke, *An Essay Concerning Human Understanding,* II, xi, 17.
39.   David Hume, *An Inquiry Concerning Human Understanding* (1748; New York, 1955), p. 16 (emphasis mine). A similar setup is noted in Descartes by Maurice Merleau-Ponty, where space is a "network of relations between objects such as would be seen by a witness to my vision or by a geometer looking over it and reconstructing it from the outside." "Eye and Mind," *The Primacy of Perception,* ed. James M. Edie (Evanston, Ill., 1964), p. 178. Jacques Lacan discusses Cartesian thought in terms of the formula "I see myself seeing myself," in *Four Fundamental Concepts of Psycho-Analysis,* pp. 80–81.
40.   Locke, *An Essay Concerning Human Understanding,* II,iii,1.

between exterior world and interior representation and to exclude anything disorderly or unruly. Reflective introspection overlaps with a regime of self-discipline.

It is in this context that Richard Rorty asserts that Locke and Descartes describe an observer fundamentally different from anything in Greek and medieval thought. For Rorty, the achievement of these two thinkers was "the conception of the human mind as an inner space in which both pains and clear and distinct ideas passed in review before an Inner Eye. . . . The novelty was the notion of a single inner space in which bodily and perceptual sensations . . . were objects of quasi-observation."[41]

In this sense Locke can be linked with Descartes. In the *Second Meditation,* Descartes asserts that "perception, or the action by which we perceive, is not a vision . . . but is solely an inspection by the mind."[42] He goes on to challenge the notion that one knows the world by means of eyesight: "It is possible that I do not even have eyes with which to see anything."[43] For Descartes, one knows the world "uniquely by perception of the mind," and the secure positioning of the self within an empty interior space is a precondition for knowing the outer world. The space of the camera obscura, its enclosedness, its darkness, its separation from an exterior, incarnate Descartes's "I will now shut my eyes, I shall stop my ears, I shall disregard my senses."[44] The orderly and calculable penetration of light rays through the single opening of the camera corresponds to the flooding of the mind by the light of reason, not the potentially dangerous dazzlement of the senses by the light of the sun.

There are two paintings by Vermeer in which the paradigm of the Cartesian camera obscura is lucidly represented.[45] Consider *The Geographer*

41.   Richard Rorty, *Philosophy and the Mirror of Nature* (Princeton, 1979), pp. 49–50. For an opposing view, see John W. Yolton, *Perceptual Acquaintance from Descartes to Reid* (Minneapolis, 1984), pp. 222–223.
42.   René Descartes, *The Philosophical Writings of Descartes,* 2 vols., trans. John Cottingham, Robert Stoothoff, and Dugald Murdoch (Cambridge, 1984), vol. 2, p. 21.
43.   Descartes, *Philosophical Writings,* vol. 2, p. 21.
44.   Descartes, *Philosophical Writings,* vol. 2, p. 24.
45.   My discussion of Vermeer clearly does not engage any of the extensive art historical speculation about his possible use of the camera obscura in the making of his pictures (see references in footnote 1). Did he in fact use one, and if so, how did it affect the makeup of his paintings? While these are interesting questions for specialists, I am not concerned here with the answers one way or the other. Such investigations tend to reduce the prob-

Vermeer. The Astronomer. *1668*.

Vermeer. The Geographer. *c. 1668–69.*

and *The Astronomer,* both painted around 1668. Each image depicts a solitary male figure absorbed in learned pursuits within the rectangular confines of a shadowy interior, an interior punctured apparently by only a single window. The astronomer studies a celestial globe, mapped out with the constellations; the geographer has before him a nautical map. Each has his eyes averted from the aperture that opens onto the outside. The exterior world is known not by direct sensory examination but through a mental survey of its "clear and distinct" representation within the room. The somber isolation of these meditative scholars within their walled interiors is not in the least an obstacle to apprehending the world outside, for the division between interiorized subject and exterior world is a pre-given condition of knowledge about the latter. The paintings then are a consummate demonstration of the reconciling function of the camera obscura: its interior is the interface between Descartes's absolutely dissimilar *res cogitans* and *res extensa,* between observer and world.[46] The camera, or room, is the site within which an orderly projection of the world, of extended substance, is made available for inspection by the mind. The production of the camera is always a projection onto a two-dimensional surface—here maps, globes, charts, and images. Each of the thinkers, in a rapt stillness, ponders that crucial feature of the world, its extension, so mysteriously unlike the unextended immediacy of their own thoughts yet rendered intelligible to mind by the clarity of these representations, by their magnitudinal relations. Rather than opposed by the objects of their study, the earth and the heavens, the geographer and the astronomer engage in a common enterprise of observing aspects of a single indivisible exterior.[47] Both of them

---

lem of the camera obscura to one of optical effects and utlimately painterly style. I contend that the camera obscura must be understood in terms of how it defined the position and possibilities of an observing subject; it was *not* simply a pictorial or stylistic option, one choice among others for a neutral and ahistorical subject. Even if Vermeer never touched the mechanical apparatus of the camera obscura and other factors explain his halation of highlights and accentuated perspective, his paintings are nonetheless profoundly embedded in the larger epistemological model of the camera.

46.   The affinity between Vermeer and Cartesian thought is discussed in Michel Serres, *La Traduction* (Paris, 1974), pp. 189–196.

47.   Descartes rejected the scholastic distinction between a sublunary or terrestrial world and a qualitatively different celestial realm in his *Principles of Philosophy,* first pub-

(and it may well be the same man in each painting) are figures for a primal and sovereign inwardness, for the autonomous individual ego that has appropriated to itself the capacity for intellectually mastering the infinite existence of bodies in space.

Descartes's description of the camera obscura in his *La dioptrique* (1637) contains some unusual features. Initially he makes a conventional analogy between the eye and the camera obscura:

> Suppose a chamber is shut up apart from a single hole, and a glass lens is placed in front of this hole with a white sheet stretched at a certain distance behind it so the light coming from objects outside forms images on the sheet. Now it is said that the room represents the eye; the hole the pupil; the lens the crystalline humour. . . .[48]

But before proceeding further, Descartes advises his reader to conduct a demonstration involving "taking the dead eye of a newly dead person (or, failing that, the eye of an ox or some other large animal)" and using the extracted eye as the lens in the pinhole of a camera obscura. Thus for Descartes the images observed within the camera obscura are formed by means of a disembodied cyclopean eye, detached from the observer, possibly not even a human eye. Additionally, Descartes specifies that one

> cut away the three surrounding membranes at the back so as to expose a large part of the humour without spilling any. . . . No light must enter this room except what comes through this eye, all of whose parts you know to be entirely transparent. Having done this, if you look at the white sheet you will see there, not perhaps without pleasure and wonder, a picture representing in natural perspective all the objects outside.[49]

---

lished in Holland in 1644. "Similarly, the earth and the heavens are composed of one and the same matter; and there cannot be a plurality of worlds." *The Philosophical Writings of Descartes,* vol. 1, p. 232. Cf. Arthur K. Wheelock, *Vermeer* (New York, 1988), Abrams, p. 108.
48.   Descartes, *The Philosophical Writings of Descartes,* vol. 1, p. 166; *Oeuvres philosophiques,* vol. 1, pp. 686–687.
49.   Descartes, *The Philosophical Writings,* vol. 1, p. 166.

By this radical disjunction of eye from observer and its installation in this formal apparatus of objective representation, the dead, perhaps even bovine eye
undergoes a kind of apotheosis and rises to an incorporeal status.[50] If at the
core of Descartes's method was the need to escape the uncertainties of mere
human vision and the confusions of the senses, the camera obscura is con-
gruent with his quest to found human knowledge on a purely objective view
of the world. The aperture of the camera obscura corresponds to a single,
mathematically definable point, from which the world can be logically
deduced by a progressive accumulation and combination of signs. It is a
device embodying man's position between God and the world. Founded on
laws of nature (optics) but extrapolated to a plane outside of nature, the camera obscura provides a vantage point onto the world analogous to the eye of
God.[51] It is an infallible metaphysical eye more than it is a "mechanical" eye.[52]
Sensory evidence was rejected in favor of the representations of the monocular apparatus, whose authenticity was beyond doubt.[53] Binocular disparity
is bound up in the physiological operation of human vision, and a monocular
device precludes having to theoretically reconcile the dissimilar, and thus

50.   See the chapter "L'oeil de boeuf: Descartes et l'après-coup idéologique," in Sarah
Kofman, *Camera obscura de l'idéologie,* pp. 71–76.
51.   Classical science privileges a description as objective "to the extent that the observer
is excluded and the description is made from a point lying de jure outside the world, that
is, from the divine viewpoint to which the human soul, created as it was in God's image,
had access at the beginning. Thus classical science still aims at discovering the unique truth
about the world, the one language that will decipher the whole of nature." Ilya Prigogine
and Isabelle Stengers, *Order Out of Chaos: Man's New Dialogue with Nature* (New York,
1984), p. 52.
52.   On Descartes's fear of the distorting power of perspective, see Karsten Harries, "Descartes, Perspective, and the Angelic Eye," *Yale French Studies* no. 49 (1973), pp. 28–42. See
also Paul Ricoeur, "The Question of the Subject: The Challenge of Semiology," in his *The
Conflict of Interpretations,* trans. Don Ihde (Evanston, Ill., 1974), pp. 236–266. Cartesian
thought, for Ricoeur, "is contemporaneous with a vision of the world in which the whole
of objectivity is spread out like a spectacle on which the *cogito* casts its sovereign gaze" (p.
236).
53.   The theological dimension of monocularity is suggested in Daniel Defoe, *The Con-
solidator: or, Memoirs of sundry transactions from the world in the moon* (London, 1705),
p. 57: "A generation have risen up, who to solve the difficulties of supernatural systems,
imagine a mighty vast something who has no form but what represents him to them as one
Great Eye. This infinite Optik they imagine to be Natura Naturans . . . the soul of man therefore, in the opinion of these naturalists, is one vast Optik Power . . . From hence they resolve
all Beings to Eyes."

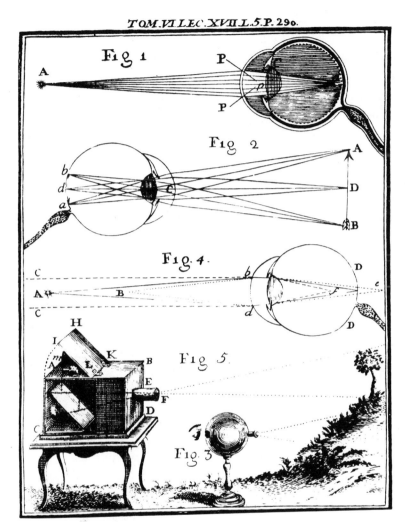

Comparison of eye and camera obscura. Early eighteenth century.

provisional, images presented to each eye. Descartes assumed that the pineal gland exercised a crucial monocular power: "There must necessarily be some place where the two images coming through the eyes . . . can come together in a single image or impression before reaching the soul, so that they do not present to it two objects instead of one."[54] At the same time, Descartes's instructions about removing the ocular membranes from the body of the eye is an operation ensuring the primal transparency of the camera obscura, of escaping from the latent opacity of the human eye.

But perhaps it is misleading to pose the vantage point of the camera as fully analogous to a divine eye. It is important that the camera obscura be understood within the context of a distinctly post-Copernican framework, within a world from which an absolutely privileged point had vanished and in which "visibility became a contingent fact."[55] It is Leibniz, along with Pascal, for whom the loss of such a point is a central problem. At the core of Leibniz's thought was the goal of reconciling the validity of universal truths with the inescapable fact of a world consisting of multiple points of view. The monad became, for Leibniz, an expression of a fragmented and decentered world, of the absence of an omniscient point of view, of the fact that every position implied a fundamental relativity that was never a problem for Descartes. At the same time, however, Leibniz insisted that each monad had the capacity to reflect in itself the whole universe from its own finite viewpoint. The conceptual structure of the camera obscura is a parallel reconciliation of a limited (or monadic) viewpoint and, at the same time, necessary truth.

54.   *The Philosophical Writings of Descartes,* vol. 1, p. 340. For Jean-François Lyotard, monocularity is one of the many Western codes and procedures through which reality is constituted according to organized constants. He outlines a visual world that is subjected to continual "correction," "flattening," and elimination of irregularities in order for a unified space to emerge. See *Discours, Figure* (Paris, 1971), esp. pp. 155–160.
55.   Hans Blumenberg, *The Legitimacy of the Modern Age,* trans. Robert M. Wallace (Cambridge, Mass., 1983), p. 371. "The Copernican revolution is based on the idea of an alliance between God and man, an idea characteristic of Renaissance Neoplatonism. . . . The fact that man has been expelled from the center of the universe in no way impedes faith in this alliance. *De revolutionibus* never speaks of this as a humiliation, and later Kepler never stopped praising the decentering of the earth: its orbit was for him the best possible vantage point for viewing the universe." Fernand Hallyn, *The Poetic Structure of the World: Copernicus and Kepler,* trans. Donald Leslie (New York, 1990), p. 282.

Leibniz, writing around 1703, seems generally to have accepted Locke's model of the camera obscura, but with the pivotal distinction that it is not a passive, receiving device but is endowed with an inherent capacity for structuring the ideas it receives:

> To increase this resemblance [between observer and dark room] we should have to postulate that there is a screen in this dark room to receive the species, and that it is not uniform but is diversified by folds representing items of innate knowledge; and, what is more, that this screen or membrane, being under tension, has a kind of elasticity or active force, and indeed that it acts (or reacts) in ways which are adapted both to past folds and to new ones.[56]

For Leibniz the camera obscura as an optical system was defined by its functional relation to a cone of vision, in which the point of the cone defined the monadic point of view. As Michel Serres has demonstrated at length:

> The science of conic sections shows that there exists a single point from which an apparent disorder can be organized into a harmony. . . . For a given plurality, for a given disorder there only exists one point around which everything can be placed in order; this point exists and it is unique. From anywhere else disorder and indetermination remain. From then on, to know a plurality of things consists in discovering the point from which their disorder can be resolved, *uno intuito,* into a unique law of order.[57]

The relation to a cone of rays is what distinguishes monadic perception from the divine point of view, which would be more properly a cylinder of rays. For Leibniz, "The difference between the appearance of a body for us and for God is the difference between scenography and ichnography" (that is, between

56.   G. W. Leibniz, *New Essays on Human Understanding* (1765), trans. Peter Remnant and Jonathan Bennett (Cambridge, 1981), p. 144. Gilles Deleuze discusses the camera obscura in relation to baroque architecture: "The monad is the autonomy of the interior, an interior without exterior." In *Le pli: Leibniz et le Baroque* (Paris, 1988), p. 39.
57.   Michel Serres, *Le Système de Leibniz et ses modèles mathématiques* (Paris, 1968), vol. 1, p. 244.

perspective and a bird's-eye view).[58] One of the most vivid examples of this scenographic perspective is in the *Monadology*:

> Just as the same city regarded from different sides offers quite different aspects, and thus appears multiplied by the perspective, so it also happens that the infinite multitude of simple substances creates the appearance of as many different universes. Yet they are but perspectives of a single universe, varied according to the points of view, which differ in each monad.[59]

One could consider two essentially different approaches to the representation of a city as models of Leibniz's distinction between scenography and ichnography. On one hand, Jacopo de' Barbari's *View of Venice* from 1500 exemplifies a pre-Copernican, synoptic and totalizing apprehension of the city as a unified entity.[60] It is a view completely outside the epistemological and technological conditions of the camera obscura. On the other hand, the mid-eighteenth century views of Venice by Canaletto, for example, disclose a field occupied by a monadic observer, within a city that is knowable only as the accumulation of multiple and diverse points of view.[61] The career of Canaletto was bound up in a discipline of the scenographic; he was trained as a stage designer, was preoccupied with the theatricality of the city, and made use of the camera obscura.[62] Whether it is a question of the stage, urban design, or visual imagery, the intelligibility of a given site depends on a precisely spec-

58.   Letter to des Bosses, Feb. 5, 1712, quoted in Serres, *Le Système de Leibniz,* vol. 1, p. 153. Louis Marin discusses the relation between ichnographic representation and royal power in *Portrait of the King,* trans. Martha Houle (Minneapolis, 1988), pp. 169–179.
59.   G. W. Leibniz, *Monadology and Other Philosophical Essays,* trans. Paul Schrecker (Indianapolis, 1965), p. 157.
60.   For an important discussion of this image see Juergen Schulz, "Jacopo de' Barbari's View of Venice: Map Making, City Views, and Moralized Geography Before the Year 1500," *Art Bulletin* 60 (1978), pp. 425–474.
61.   "The baroque city, on the contrary, presents itself as an open texture without reference to a privileged signifier that gives it orientation and meaning." Severo Sarduy, *Barroco* (Paris, 1975), pp. 63–64.
62.   For Canaletto's use of the camera obscura, see Terisio Pignatti, *Il quaderno di diseqni del Canaletto alle Gallerie di Venezia* (Milan, 1958), pp. 20–22; André Corboz, *Canaletto: una Venezia immaginaria,* vol. 1 (Milan, 1985), pp. 143–154; and W. G. Constable and J. G. Links, *Canaletto,* vol. 1 (Oxford, 1976), pp. 161–163.

Jacopo de' Barbari. View of Venice *(detail). 1500.*

ified relation between a delimited point of view and a tableau.[63] The camera obscura, with its monocular aperture, became a more perfect terminus for a cone of vision, a more perfect incarnation of a single point than the awkward binocular body of the human subject. The camera, in a sense, was a metaphor for the most rational possibilities of a perceiver within the increasingly dynamic disorder of the world.

63.   Hélène Leclerc insists that by the mid-seventeenth century, beginning with the career of Bernini, a related concept of scenography traverses theatre, urban design, architecture, and visual imagery, in "La Scène d'illusion et l'hégémonie du théâtre à l'italienne," in *Histoire des Spectacles,* ed. Guy Dumur (Paris, 1965), pp. 581–624.

Antonio Canaletto. Piazza San Marco, looking east from the northwest corner. c. 1755.

Although Bishop Berkeley's work on vision does not discuss the camera obscura, his model of perception coincides with that presupposed by the camera. In *The Theory of Vision Vindicated* (1732), he demonstrates his familiarity with contemporary treatises on perspective:

> We may suppose a diaphanous plain erected near the eye, perpendicular to the horizon, and divided into small equal squares. A straight line from the eye to the utmost limit of the horizon, passing through this diaphanous plain, as projected or represented in the perpendicular plain, would rise. The eye sees all the parts and objects in the horizontal plain through certain corresponding squares of the perpendicular diaphanous phrase. . . . It is true this diaphanous plain, and the images supposed to be projected thereon, are altogether of a tangible nature: But then there are pictures relative to those images: and those pictures have an order among themselves.[64]

Even though the architectural enclosure of the camera obscura is absent, the observer here is still one who observes a projection onto a field exterior to himself, and Berkeley explicitly describes the ordered surface of this field as a grid on which the universal grammar, "the language of the Author of nature," could be known. But whether it is Berkeley's divine signs of God arrayed on a diaphanous plane, Locke's sensations "imprinted" on a white page, or Leibniz's elastic screen, the eighteenth-century observer confronts a unified space of order, unmodified by his or her own sensory and physiological apparatus, on which the contents of the world can be studied and compared, known in terms of a multitude of relationships. In Rorty's words, "It is as if the *tabula rasa* were perpetually under the gaze of the unblinking Eye of the Mind . . . it becomes obvious that the imprinting is of less interest than the observation of the imprint—all the knowing gets done, so to speak, by the Eye which observes the imprinted tablet, rather than by the tablet itself."[65]

For Heidegger, Descartes's work inaugurates "the age of the world picture," but the picture to which Heidegger refers does not imply a new priority

64.   George Berkeley, *The Theory of Vision Vindicated,* in *The Works of George Berkeley Bishop of Cloyne,* ed. A. A. Luce and T. E. Jessop (London, 1948–1957), vol. 1, pp. 270–271.
65.   Rorty, *Philosophy and the Mirror of Nature,* pp. 143–144.

given to the sense of vision. Rather, "what belongs to the essence of the picture is standing-together, system . . . a unity that develops out of the projection of the objectivity of whatever is."[66] This is the same unity of the camera obscura, a field of projection corresponding to the space of Descartes's *mathesis univ-ersalis,* in which all objects of thought, "irrespective of subject matter," can be ordered and compared: "Our project being, not to inspect the isolated natures of things, but to compare them with each other so that some may be known on the basis of others."[67]

The unity of this ground on which everything may be arranged in common finds one of its fullest expressions in the pages of the *Encyclopédie.* According to Michel Foucault, the great project of this thought is an exhaustive ordering of the world characterized by "discovery of simple elements and their progressive combination; and at their center they form a table on which knowledge is displayed contemporary with itself. The center of knowledge in the seventeenth and eighteenth centuries is the *table.*"[68] Ernst Cassirer's read-ing of the Enlightenment, though unfashionable now, more than echoes cer-tain parts of Foucault's construction of "classical thought." While much Anglo-American intellectual history tends to pose an atomization of cognition in this period, Cassirer sees a Leibnizian underpinning to eighteenth-century thought:

> With the advent of the eighteenth-century the absolutism of the unity principle seems to lose its grip and to accept some limitations or concessions. But these modifications do not touch the core of the thought itself. For the function of unification continues to be recognized as the basic role of reason. Rational order and control of the data of experience are not possible without strict unification. To "know" a manifold of experience is to place its component parts in such a relationship to one another that, starting from a given point, we can run through them according to a constant and gen-

---

66.   Martin Heidegger, "The Age of the World Picture," in *The Question Concerning Tech-nology and Other Essays,* trans. William Lovitt (New York, 1977), pp. 115–54.
67.   Descartes, "Rules for the Direction of the Mind," in *Philosophical Writings,* pp. 19, 21.
68.   Michel Foucault, *The Order of Things* (New York, 1970), pp. 74–75. On Leibniz and the table, see Gilles Deleuze, *Le pli,* p. 38.

eral rule . . . the unknown and the known participate in a "common nature."[69]

Cassirer might well have agreed with Foucault that observation in the seventeenth and eighteenth centuries is "a perceptible knowledge."[70] But it is hardly a knowledge that is organized exclusively around visuality. Although the dominance of the camera obscura paradigm does in fact imply a privilege given to vision, it is a vision that is *a priori* in the service of a nonsensory faculty of understanding that alone gives a true conception of the world. It would be completely misleading to pose the camera obscura as an early stage in an ongoing autonomization and specialization of vision that continues into the nineteenth and twentieth centuries. Vision can be privileged at different historical moments in ways that simply are not continuous with one another. Situating subjectivity within a monolithic Western tradition of scopic or specular power effaces and subsumes the singular and incommensurable procedures and regimes through which an observer has been constituted.[71]

For example, Berkeley's theory of perception is based on the essential dissimilarity of the senses of vision and touch, but this insistence on the heterogeneity of the senses is remote from nineteenth-century notions of the autonomy of vision and the separation of the senses.[72] Berkeley is hardly alone

---

69.   Ernst Cassirer, *The Philosophy of the Enlightenment,* trans. Fritz Koelln and James P. Pettegrove (Princeton, 1951), p. 23. An alternative continental reading of this aspect of eighteenth-century thought is Max Horkheimer and Theodor Adorno, *Dialectic of Enlightenment,* trans. John Cumming (New York, 1979). For them, the quantitative "unity" of Enlightenment thought was continuous with and a precondition for the technocratic domination of the twentieth century. "In advance, the Enlightenment recognized as being and occurrence only what can be apprehended in unity: its ideal is the system from which all and everything follows. Its rationalist and empiricist versions do not part company on that point. Even though the individual schools may interpret the axioms differently, the structure of scientific unity has always been the same. . . . The multiplicity of forms is reduced to position and arrangement, history to fact, things to matter" (p. 7).

70.   Foucault, *The Order of Things,* p. 132. On the problem of perception in Condillac and Diderot, see Suzanne Gearhart, *Open Boundary of Fiction and History: A Critical Approach to the French Enlightenment* (Princeton, 1984), pp. 161–199.

71.   See Martin Jay, "Scopic Regimes of Modernity," in *Vision and Visuality,* ed. Hal Foster (Seattle, 1988), pp. 3–27.

72.   Anglo-American criticism often tends to posit a continuous development of eighteenth-century thought into nineteenth-century empiricism and associationism. A typical account is Maurice Mandelbaum, *History, Man and Reason: A Study in Nineteenth Century Thought* (Baltimore, 1971, especially pp. 147–162. After insisting on a continuity between

in the eighteenth century in his concern with achieving a fundamental har-
monization of the senses, in which a key model for visual perception is the
sense of touch. The Molyneux problem, which so preoccupied the thought of
the eighteenth century, poses the case of a perceiver who is ignorant of one
of the languages of the senses, namely sight. The best known formulation of
the problem is Locke's:

> Suppose a man born blind, and now adult, and taught by his touch
> to distinguish between a cube and a sphere of the same metal, and
> nighly of the same bigness, so as to tell, when he felt one and the
> other, which is the cube, which the sphere. Suppose then the cube
> and sphere placed on a table, and the blind man be made to see:
> *quaere,* whether *by his sight before he touched them,* he could now
> distinguish and tell which is the globe, which the cube?[73]

But regardless of how the problem was ultimately answered, whether the
claim was nativist or empiricist, the testimony of the senses constituted for the
eighteenth century a common surface of order.[74] The problem quite simply
was how the passage from one order of sense perception to another took

---

the thought of Locke, Condillac, and Hartley and nineteenth-century associationism, Mandelbaum concedes, "Thus, in its origins, associationism was not what James Mill and Alexander Bain later sought to make of it, a full-blown psychological system, serving to classify
and relate all aspects of mental life; it was, rather, a principle used to connect a general
epistemological position with more specific issues of intellectual and practical concern.
Among these issues, questions concerning the foundations of morality and the relations of
morality to religion had an especially important place" (p. 156). However, what Mandelbaum terms "a general epistemological position" is precisely the relative unity of Enlightenment knowledge onto which he imposes the separations and categories of the thought
of his own time. Religion, morality and epistemology did not exist as discrete and separate
domains.

73.   John Locke, *An Essay Concerning Human Understanding,* II, ix, 8.

74.   For example, see Thomas Reid, *Essays on the Powers of the Human Mind* [1785]
(Edinburgh, 1819), vol. 2, pp. 115–116: "If any thing more were necessary to be said on a
point so evident, we might observe, that if the faculty of seeing were in the eye, that of hearing in the ear, and so of the other senses, the necessary consequence of this would be, that
the thinking principle, which I call myself, is not one but many. But this is contrary to the
irresistable conviction of every man. When I say, I see, I hear, I feel, I remember, this implies
that it is one and the same self that performs all these operations."

place.[75] Or for Condillac, in his famed discussion of the senses coming to life one by one in his statue, the problem was how the senses could "reconvene," that is, come together in the perceiver.[76]

But for those whose answers to Molyneux were, in one way or another, negative—a blind man suddenly restored with sight would *not* immediately recognize the objects before him—and these included Locke, Berkeley, Diderot, Condillac, and others, they share little with the physiologists and psychologists of the nineteenth century who were also, with greater scientific authority, to answer the question negatively. By insisting that knowledge, and specifically knowledge of space and depth, is built up out of an orderly accumulation and cross-referencing of perceptions on a plane independent of the viewer, eighteenth-century thought could know nothing of the ideas of pure visibility to arise in the nineteenth century. Nothing could be more removed from Berkeley's theory of how distance is perceived than the science of the stereoscope. This quintessentially nineteenth-century device, with which tangibility (or relief) is constructed solely through an organization of *optical* cues (and the amalgamation of the observer into a component of the apparatus), eradicates the very field on which eighteenth-century knowledge arranged itself.

From Descartes to Berkeley to Diderot, vision is conceived in terms of analogies to the senses of touch.[77] Diderot's work will be misunderstood if we do not see at the outset how deeply ambivalent he was toward vision, and how he resisted treating any phenomenon in terms of a single sense.[78] His *Letters on the Blind* (1749), in its account of Nicholas Saunderson, a blind mathematician, asserts the possibility of a tactile geometry, and that touch as well as sight carries with it the capacity for apprehending universally valid truths. The

75.   See Cassirer, *The Philosophy of the Enlightenment,* p. 108. For recent discussions of the problem, see M. J. Morgan, *Molyneux's Question: Vision, Touch and the Philosohy of Perception* (Cambridge, 1977); and Francine Markovits, "Mérian, Diderot et l'aveugle," in J.-B. Mérian, *Sur le problème de Molyneux* (Paris, 1984), pp. 193–282.

76.   Etienne de Condillac, "Traité des sensations" (1754), in *Oeuvres philosophiques de Condillac,* vol. 1, ed. Georges Le Roy (Paris, 1947–1951).

77.   See Michel Serres, *Hermès ou la communication* (Paris, 1968), pp. 124–125; and Maurice Merleau-Ponty, *The Primacy of Perception,* ed. James M. Edie (Evanston, Ill., 1964), pp. 169–172.

78.   On Diderot's attitude toward the senses, see Elisabeth de Fontenay, *Diderot: Reason and Resonance,* trans. Jeffrey Mehlman (New York, 1982), pp. 157–169.

essay is not so much a depreciation of the sense of vision as it is a refutation of its exclusivity. Diderot details Saunderson's devices for calculation and demonstration, rectangular wooden boards with built-in grids marked out by raised pins. by connecting the pins with silk threads Saunderson's fingers could trace out and read an infinity of figures and their relations, all calculable by their location on the demarcated grid. Here the Cartesian table appears in another form, but its underlying status is the same. The certainty of knowledge did not depend solely on the eye but on a more general relation of a unified human sensorium to a delimited space of order on which positions could be known and compared.[79] In a sighted person the senses are dissimilar, but through what Diderot calls "reciprocal assistance" they provide knowledge about the world.

Yet despite this discourse on the senses and sensation, we are still within the same epistemological field occupied by the camera obscura and its overriding of the immediate subjective evidence of the body. Even in Diderot, a so-called materialist, the senses are conceived more as adjuncts of a rational mind and less as physiological organs. Each sense operates according to an immutable semantic logic that transcends its mere physical mode of functioning. Thus the significance of the image discussed in Diderot's *Letters on the Blind*: a blindfolded man in an outdoor space steps forward, tentatively holding a stick in each hand, extended to feel the objects and area before him. But paradoxically this is *not* an image of a man literally blind; rather it is an abstract diagram of a fully sighted observer, in which vision operates like the sense of touch. Just as the eyes are not finally what see, however, so the carnal organs of touch are also disengaged from contact with an exterior world. Of this blind and prosthesis-equipped figure that illustrated Descartes's *La dioptrique* Diderot remarks, "Neither Descartes nor those who have followed him have been able to give a clearer conception of vision."[80] This anti-optical

79.   On the persistence of Cartesianism in Enlightenment thought, see Aram Vartanian, *Diderot and Descartes: A Study of Scientific Naturalism in the Enlightenment* (Princeton: 1953).
80.   Diderot asserts that the person most capable of theorizing on vision and the senses would be "a philosopher who had profoundly meditated on the subject in the dark, or to adopt the language of the poets, one who had put out his eyes in order to be better acquainted with vision." *Lettres sur les aveugles,* in *Oeuvres philosophiques,* p. 87.

Illustration from 1724 edition of Descartes's La dioptrique.

notion of sight pervaded the work of other thinkers during both the seventeenth and eighteenth centuries: for Berkeley there is no such thing as visual
perception of depth, and Condillac's statue effectively masters space with the
help of movement and touch. The notion of vision as touch is adequate to a
field of knowledge whose contents are organized as stable positions within
an extensive terrain. But in the nineteenth century such a notion became
incompatible with a field organized around exchange and flux, in which a
knowledge bound up in touch would have been irreconcilable with the centrality of mobile signs and commodities whose identity is exclusively optical.
The stereoscope, as I will show, became a crucial indication of the remapping
and subsumption of the tactile within the optical.

The paintings of J.-B. Chardin are lodged within these same questions
of knowledge and perception. His still lifes, especially, are a last great presentation of the classical object in all its plenitude, before it is sundered irrevocably into exchangeable and ungrounded signifiers or into the painterly
traces of an autonomous vision. The slow-burning glow of Chardin's late
work, an effulgence inseparable from use values, is a light soon to be eclipsed
in the nineteenth century, either by the synthetic aura of the commodity or by
the radiance of an artwork whose very survival demanded a denial of its mere
objectivity. In his still-lifes, with their shallow, stage-like ledges populated with
forms, to know something was not to behold the optical singularity of an
object but to apprehend its fuller phenomenal identity simultaneously with
its position on an ordered field. The aesthetic imperative by which Chardin
systematizes the simple forms of everyday use and of sensory experience is
close to Diderot's insistence on representing nature in its variability and flux,
while at the same time deriving from that shifting knowledge universally valid
ideas.[81]

Take, for example, Chardin's *Basket of Wild Strawberries* from around
1761. His superb cone of stacked strawberries is a sign of how rational knowledge of geometrical form can coincide with a perceptual intuition of the multiplicity and perishability of life. For Chardin, sensory knowledge and rational
knowledge are inseparable. His work is both the product of empirical knowl-

81.   See Diderot, *Le Rêve de D'Alembert,* in *Oeuvres philosophiques,* pp. 299–313.

J.-B. Chardin. Basket of Wild Strawberries. *1761.*

edge about the contingent specificity of forms, their position within a world of social meanings, and at the same time an ideal structure founded on a deductive rational clarity. But the immediacy of sense experience is transposed to a scenic space within which the relation of one object to another has less to do with sheer optical appearances than with knowledge of isomorphisms and positions on a unified terrain. It is in the context of the Cartesian table that we should read Chardin's enumerative clarity, his groupings of objects into sets and subsets. These formal analogies are not about a surface design, but rather a permanent space across which are distributed "the non-quantitative identities and differences that separated and united things."[82]

82.   Foucault, *The Order of Things,* p. 218.

Chardin's painting is also part of the eighteenth-century preoccupation with ensuring transparency over opacity. Newtonian and Cartesian physics, notwithstanding the large divide between them, both sought to confirm the unity of a single homogeneous field in spite of the diversity of media and possibilities of refraction within it. Dioptrics (science of refraction) was of greater interest to the eighteenth century than catoptrics (reflection), and this predeliction is most obviously evident in Newton's *Opticks*.[83] It was crucial that the distorting power of a medium, whether a lens, air, or liquid, be neutralized, and this could be done if the properties of that medium were mastered intellectually and thus rendered effectively transparent through the exercise of reason. In Chardin's *Boy Blowing Bubbles,* from around 1739, a glass filled with dull soapy liquid stands at one side of a shallow ledge, while a youth with a straw transforms that formless liquid opacity into the transparent sphere of a soap bubble situated symmetrically over the rectilinear ledge. This depicted act of effortless mastery, in which vision and touch work cooperatively (and this occurs in many of his images), is paradigmatic of Chardin's own activity as an artist. His apprehension of the coidentity of idea and matter and their finely set positions within a unified field discloses a thought for which haptic and optic are not autonomous terms but together constitute an indivisible mode of knowledge.

Thus the flickering heaviness of the atmosphere in Chardin's mature work is a medium in which vision performs like the sense of touch, passing through a space of which no fraction is empty.[84] Far from being an airless Newtonian realm, the world of Chardin's art is adjacent to a Cartesian science of a corpuscular, matter-filled reality in which there is no void, no action at a distance. And if the apocryphal stories of Chardin painting with his fingers are to be put to use, it should not be in the service of privileging timeless "painterly"

83.   On the modernity of dioptrics, see Molyneux, *Dioptrica nova,* pp. 251–252. "No one denies the ancients the knowledge of Catoptricks . . . yet certainly Optick-Glasses are a modern invention."

84.   See Diderot, *Oeuvres esthétiques,* ed. Paul Vernière (Paris, 1968), p. 484. See also Joseph Addison, *The Spectator,* ed. Donald F. Bond (Oxford, 1965), no. 411, June 21, 1712: "Our sight . . . may be considered as a more delicate and diffusive Kind of Touch, that spreads its self over an infinite Multitude of Bodies."

J.-B. Chardin. Boy Blowing Bubbles. *1739*.

values but rather to underscore the primacy of a vision, belonging to a specific historical moment, in which tactility was fully embedded.[85]

Chardin is at a vast remove from an artist like Cézanne. If Chardin is understandable in the context of the Molyneux problem and the coordination of sensory languages, Cézanne implies not just the possibility of achieving the state of a blind man suddenly restored to sight, but more importantly of retaining this "innocence" permanently. In the seventeenth and eighteenth centuries this kind of "primordial" vision simply could not be thought, even as a hypothetical possibility. In all the speculation surrounding the 1728 case of the Chesleden boy, no one was ever to suggest that a blind person restored to sight would initially see a luminous and somehow self-sufficient revelation of colored patches.[86] Instead, that inaugural moment of vision was a void that could not be spoken of or represented, because it was empty of discourse and thus of meaning. Vision for the newly sighted person took shape when words, uses, and locations could be assigned to objects. If Cézanne, Ruskin, Monet, or any other artist of the nineteenth century is able to conceive of an "innocence of the eye," it is only because of a major reconfiguration of the observer earlier in that century.

85.   See the discussion of Chardin's technique in Norman Bryson, *Word and Image: French Painting of the Ancien Regime* (Cambridge, 1981), pp. 118–119. On the relation between Rembrandt's touch and Cartesian optics, see Svetlana Alpers, *Rembrandt's Enterprise: The Studio and the Market* (Chicago, 1988), pp. 22–24. My reading of a cooperative, reciprocal relation between vision and touch in Chardin as a model of sensory attentiveness can be related to Michael Fried's notion of absorption articulated in his groundbreaking *Absorption and Theatricality: Painting and Beholder in the Age of Diderot* (Berkeley, 1980).
86.   In 1728 the surgeon Cheselden performed a successful cataract operation on a fourteen-year-old boy blind from birth. See Diderot, *Lettres sur les aveugles*, p. 319; and Berkeley, *Theory of Vision Vindicated*, sec. 71. See also Jeffrey Mehlman, *Cataract: A Study in Diderot* (Middletown, Conn., 1979).

3   Subjective Vision and the Separation of the Senses

> *To admit untruth as a condition
> of life—this does indeed imply a ter-
> rible negation of the customary
> valuations.*
>
> —Friedrich Nietzsche

> *Being composed of a plurality of
> irreducible forces the body is a mul-
> tiplicity, its unity is that of a mul-
> tiple phenomenon, a "unity of
> domination."*
>
> —Gilles Deleuze

One of the opening paragraphs of Goethe's *Farbenlehre* (1810) begins with the following account:

> Let a room be made as dark as possible; let there be a circular open-
> ing in the window shutter about three inches in diameter, which
> may be closed or not at pleasure. The sun being suffered to shine
> through this on a white surface, let the spectator from some little
> distance fix his eyes on this bright circle thus admitted.[1]

---

1.   Johann Wolfgang von Goethe, *Theory of Colours*, trans. Charles Eastlake (1840; Cambridge, Mass., 1970), pp. 16–17.

Goethe, following a long established practice, has made a camera obscura the site of his optical studies. Again, much as it had in Newton's *Opticks,* the dark room seems to establish categorical relations between interior and exterior, between light source and aperture, and between observer and object. As Goethe continues his recitation, however, he abruptly and stunningly abandons the order of the camera obscura:

> The hole being then closed, let him look towards the darkest part of the room; a circular image will now be seen to float before him. The middle of the circle will appear bright, colourless, or somewhat yellow, but the border will appear red. After a time this red, increasing towards the centre, covers the whole circle, and at last the bright central point. No sooner, however, is the whole circle red than the edge begins to be blue, and the blue gradually encroaches inwards on the red. When the whole is blue the edge becomes dark and colourless. The darker edge again slowly encroaches on the blue till the whole circle appears colourless. . . .[2]

Goethe's instruction to seal the hole, "Man schliesse darauf die Offnung," announces a disordering and negation of the camera obscura as both an optical system and epistemological figure. The closing off of the opening dissolves the distinction between inner and outer space on which the very functioning of the camera (as apparatus and paradigm) depended. But it is now not simply a question of an observer repositioned in a sealed interior to view its particular contents; the optical experience described here by Goethe presents a notion of vision that the classical model was incapable of encompassing.

The colored circles that seem to float, undulate, and undergo a sequence of chromatic transformations have no correlative either within or without the dark room; as Goethe explains at length, they are "physiological" colors belonging entirely to the body of the observer and are "the necessary conditions of vision."

> Let the observer look steadfastly on a small coloured object and let it be taken away after a time while his eyes remain unmoved; the

2.   Goethe, *Theory of Colours*, p. 17. Emphasis added.

spectrum of another colour will then be visible on the white plane
. . . it arises from an image which now *belongs to the eye.*[3]

The corporeal subjectivity of the observer, which was a priori excluded from the concept of the camera obscura, suddenly becomes the site on which an observer is possible. The human body, in all its contingency and specificity, generates "the spectrum of another colour," and thus becomes the active producer of optical experience.

The ramifications of Goethe's color theory are manifold and have little to do with the empirical "truth" of his assertions or the "scientific" character of his experiments.[4] Contained within his unsystematized accumulation of statements and findings is a key delineation of subjective vision, a post-Kantian notion that is both a product and constituent of modernity. What is important about Goethe's account of subjective vision is the inseparability of two models usually presented as distinct and irreconcilable: a physiological observer who will be described in increasing detail by the empirical sciences in the nineteenth century, *and* an observer posited by various "romanticisms" and early modernisms as the active, autonomous producer of his or her own visual experience.

Clearly Kant's "Copernican revolution" (*Drehung*) of the spectator, proposed in the preface to the second edition of the *Critique of Pure Reason* (1787), is a definitive sign of a new organization and positioning of the subject. For Kant, continuing the use of optical figures, it is "a change in point of view," such that "our representation of things, as they are given, does not conform to these things as they are in themselves, but that these objects as appearances,

---

3.   Goethe, *Theory of Colours*, p. 21. See Ernst Cassirer, *Rousseau, Kant, and Goethe*, trans. James Gutmann (Princeton, 1945), pp. 81–82: In his color theory Goethe aimed "to include nothing but the world of the eye, which contains only form and color."

4.   On Goethe's optics see, especially, Dennis L. Sepper, *Goethe contra Newton: Polemics and the project for a new science of color* (Cambridge, 1988). See also Eric G. Forbes, "Goethe's Vision of Science," in *Common Denominators in Art and Science*, ed. Martin Pollock, pp. 9–15; Rudolf Magnus, *Goethe as a Scientist*, trans. Heinz Norden (New York, 1949), pp. 125–199; Neil M. Ribe, "Goethe's Critique of Newton: A Reconsideration," *Studies in the History and Philosophy of Science* 16, no. 4 (December 1985), pp. 315–335; and George A. Wells, "Goethe's Qualitative Optics," *Journal of the History of Ideas* 32 (1971), pp. 617–626.

conform to our mode of representation."⁵ William Blake put it more simply: "As the eye, such the object."⁶ Michel Foucault emphasizes that vision in the classical era was precisely the opposite of Kant's subject-centered epistemology, that it was then a form of immediate knowing, "a perceptible knowledge." For example:

> Natural history [in the 18th century] is nothing more than the nomination of the visible. Hence its apparent simplicity, and that air of naiveté it has from a distance, so simple does it appear and so obviously imposed by things themselves.⁷

In the aftermath of Kant's work there is an irreversible clouding over of the transparency of the subject-as-observer. Vision, rather than a privileged form of knowing, becomes itself an object of knowledge, of observation. From the beginning of the nineteenth century a science of vision will tend to mean increasingly an interrogation of the physiological makeup of the human subject, rather than the mechanics of light and optical transmission. It is a moment when the visible escapes from the timeless order of the camera obscura and becomes lodged in another apparatus, within the unstable physiology and temporality of the human body.

When Goethe's experiments repeatedly call for either a darkened room or, perhaps more significantly, the closed eye, he is not simply privileging an experience of being severed from contact with an external world. On one hand he is indicating his conviction that color is always the product of an admixture of light and shadow: "Colour itself is a degree of darkness; hence Kircher is perfectly right in calling it *lumen opaticum.*"⁸ On the other hand he is also posing conditions in which the inescapable physiological components of vision can be artificially isolated and made observable. For Goethe, and for Schopenhauer soon after, vision is always an irreducible complex of

5.   Immanuel Kant, *Critique of Pure Reason*, trans. Norman Kemp Smith (New York, 1965), pp. 24–25.
6.   William Blake, "Annotations to Reynolds" [c. 1808], in *Complete Writings*, ed. Geoffrey Keynes (Oxford, 1972), p. 456.
7.   Michel Foucault, *The Order of Things* (New York, 1970), p. 132.
8.   Goethe, *Theory of Colours*, p. 31.

elements belonging to the observer's body and of data from an exterior world. Thus the kind of separation between interior representation and exterior reality implicit in the camera obscura becomes in Goethe's work a single surface of affect on which interior and exterior have few of their former meanings and positions. Color, as the primary object of vision, is now atopic, cut off from any spatial referent.

Goethe insistently cites experiences in which the subjective contents of vision are dissociated from an objective world, in which the body itself produces phenomena that have no external correlate. Notions of correspondence and of reflection on which classical optics and theories of knowledge were based, although retained elsewhere by Goethe, have lost their centrality and necessity in this text. Perhaps most important is his designation of opacity as a crucial and productive component of vision. If discourse on visuality in the seventeenth and eighteenth centuries repressed and concealed whatever threatened the transparence of an optical system, Goethe signals a reversal, and instead poses the opacity of the observer as a necessary condition for the appearance of phenomena.[9] Perception occurs within the realm of what Goethe called *das Trübe*—the turbid, cloudy, or gloomy. Pure light and pure transparence are now beyond the limits of human visibility.[10]

Goethe's appeal to subjective observation is part of a shift constituting what Foucault calls "the threshold of our modernity." When the camera obscura was the dominant model of observation, it was "a form of representation which made knowledge in general possible." At the beginning of the nineteenth century, however,

> the site of analysis is no longer representation but man in his finitude. . . . It was found that knowledge has anatomo-physiological conditions, that it is formed gradually within the structures of the body, that it may have a privileged place within it, but that its forms cannot be dissociated from its peculiar functioning; in short, that

9.   The thematic of repression is central to Jean-François Lyotard's discussion of Renaissance representation in *Discours, Figure*, esp. pp. 163–189.
10.   This point is made in Eliane Escoubas, "L'oeil (du) teinturier," *Critique* 37, no. 418 (March 1982), pp. 231–242.

there is a nature of human knowledge that determines its forms
and that at the same time can be manifest to it in its own empirical
contents.[11]

Within Foucault's framework, Goethe's affirmation of the subjective and the
physiological in perception parallels the contemporary work of Maine de
Biran. During the first decade of the century, the latter outlined a science of
the *"sens intime"* in an attempt to understand more accurately the nature of
inward experience. In an extraordinary body of work that challenged the
assumptions of sensationalism and British empiricism, Maine de Biran
asserted the autonomy and primacy of interior experience (as Bergson and
Whitehead were to do much later), and postulated a fundamental difference
between internal and external impressions. What is crucial about Biran's work
in the early 1800s is the emergence of a restless, active body whose anxious
motilité (i.e., willed effort against felt resistance) was a precondition of
subjectivity.

 In seeking to grasp the density and the immediacy of the *sens intime,*
Maine de Biran blurs and often dissolves the identity of the very inwardness
that he sought to affirm. He employed the term *coenésthèse* to describe "one's
immediate awareness of the presence of the body in perception" and "the
simultaneity of a composite of impressions inhering in different parts of the
organism."[12] Visual perception, for example, is inseparable from the muscular
movements of the eye and the physical effort involved in focusing on an object
or in simply holding one's eyelids open. For Maine de Biran, the eye, like the
rest of the body, becomes a stubborn physical fact, perpetually requiring the
active exertion of force and activity. In a reversal of the classical model of the
apparatus as a neutral device of pure transmission, both the viewer's sensory
organs and their activity now are inextricably mixed with whatever object they
behold. Seven years before Goethe published the *Farbenlehre,* Maine de

11.   Michel Foucault, *The Order of Things* (New York, 1970), p. 319.
12.   Maine de Biran, *Considerations sur les principes d'une division des faits psycholo-*
giques et physiologiques, in *Oeuvres des Maine de Biran,* Vol. 13, ed. P. Tisserand (Paris,
1949), p. 180. An important study of Maine de Biran is Michel Henry, *Philosophie et phén-*
oménologie du corps: essai sur l'ontologie biranienne (Paris, 1965). Also see Aldous Huxley's meditations on the work of Maine de Biran, in *Themes and Variations* (London, 1950),
pp. 1–152.

Biran discussed how our perception of color was determined by the body's tendency to fatigue (by physiological modulation over time) and that the very process of becoming tired was in fact perception.

> When the eye fixes itself on a single color, for a certain length of time, in its manner of becoming fatigued there follows a mixed form of this color and several others, and over time the original color will no longer be contained in this new mixture.[13]

For both of them, the absolute values accorded to color by Newtonian theory are displaced by an insistence on color's transient unfolding within the human subject.

Maine de Biran is among the first of many in the nineteenth century to unravel the assumptions of Condillac and others about the composition of perception. Condillac's notion of sensation as a simple unit, a building block out of which clear perceptions were assembled, is no longer adequate to the new multilayered and temporally dispersed perception that Maine de Biran details, making impossible "a soul reduced to pure receptivity." For both Goethe and Maine de Biran, subjective observation is not the inspection of an inner space or a theater of representations. Instead, observation is increasingly exteriorized; the viewing body and its objects begin to constitute a single field on which inside and outside are confounded. Perhaps most importantly, both observer and observed are subject to the same modes of empirical study. For Georges Canguilhem, the reorganization of human knowledge at the beginning of the nineteenth century signals an end to the idea of a qualitatively different human order, and he cites the major discovery by Maine de Biran that since "the soul is necessarily incarnated, there is no psychology without biology."[14] It was the potentiality of this body that would be increasingly subjected to forms of investigation, regulation, and discipline throughout the nineteenth century.

The inseparability of psychology and biology dominates the thought of another important nineteenth-century researcher on vision. In 1815 the

13.   Maine de Biran, *Influence de l'habitude sur la faculté de penser* [1803], ed. P. Tisserand (Paris, 1953), pp. 56–60.
14.   Georges Canguilhem, "Qu'est-ce que la psychologie," *Etudes d'histoire et de philosophie des sciences* (Paris, 1968), pp. 374–375.

young Arthur Schopenhauer sent Goethe a copy of his manuscript *Über das Sehen und die Farben.*[15] The text was, in part, an homage to the older writer's battle with Newton, but it went much further than Goethe's theory in its insistence on the wholly subjective nature of vision. Schopenhauer abandoned Goethe's classification of colors into the physiological, the physical, and the chemical, eliminating the latter two categories and asserting that color could only be considered by an exclusively physiological theory. For Schopenhauer, color was synonymous with the reactions and activity of the retina; Goethe, he believed, had erred in his attempt to formulate an objective truth about color, independent of the human body.

The differences between Goethe and Schopenhauer should not, however, be overemphasized. In their common preoccupation with color, and in the emphasis they give to physiological phenomena for its explanation, they indicate a major reversal of influential eighteenth-century views on the topic, including Kant's devaluation of color in the *Critique of Judgement.*[16] Both, too, are implicated in a more general German reaction against Newtonian optics in the early nineteenth century.[17] The priority previously accorded to Lockean primary qualities over secondary qualities becomes inverted. For Locke, secondary qualities were what generated various sensations, and he insisted that they bore no resemblance to any real objects. But for Schopenhauer and for the Goethe of the *Theory of Colours,* these secondary qualities constitute our primary image of an external reality. Knowledge of a phenomenal world begins with the excited condition of the retina and develops according to the constitution of this organ. The positing of external objects, as well as concepts of shape, extension, and solidity come only after this founding experience. For Locke and other of his contemporaries, primary

15.   Arthur Schopenhauer, *Sämtliche Werke*, ed. Paul Deussen (Munich, 1911), vol. 3, pp. 1–93. A valuable assessment of this text is P. F. H. Lauxtermann, "Five Decisive Years: Schopenhauer's Epistemology as Reflected in his Theory of Color," *Studies in the History and Philosophy of Science* vol. 18, no. 3, 1987, pp. 271–291. See also Wilhelm Ostwald, *Goethe, Schopenhauer und die Farbenlehre* (Leipzig, 1931).
16.   Foucault describes vision in the eighteenth century as "a visibility freed from all other sensory burdens and restricted, moreover, to black and white." *The Order of Things*, p. 133.
17.   On Schopenhauer and the resistance to Newtonian optics, see Maurice Elie, "Introduction," in Arthur Schopenhauer, *Textes sur la vue et sur les couleurs*, trans. Maurice Elie (Paris, 1986), pp. 9–26.

qualities always bear a relation of correspondence, if not resemblance, to exterior objects, and conform to classical models of the observer, such as the camera obscura. In Schopenhauer this notion of correspondence between subject and object disappears; he studies color only with reference to sensations belonging to the body of the observer. He makes explicit the irrelevance of distinctions between interior and exterior:

> Still less can there enter into consciousness a distinction, which generally does not take place, between object and representation . . . what is immediate can only be the sensation; and this is confined to the sphere beneath our skin. This can be explained from the fact that outside us is exclusively a spatial determination, but space itself is . . . a function of our brain.[18]

Unlike Locke and Condillac, Schopenhauer rejected any model of the observer as passive receiver of sensation, and instead posed a subject who was both the site and producer of sensation. For Schopenhauer, following Goethe, the fact that color manifests itself when the observer's eyes are closed is central. He repeatedly demonstrated how "what occurs within the brain," within the subject, is wrongly apprehended as occurring outside the brain in the world. His overturning of the camera obscura model received additional confirmation from early nineteenth-century research that precisely located the blind spot as the exact point of entrance of the optic nerve on the retina. Unlike the illuminating aperture of the camera obscura, the point separating the eye and brain of Schopenhauer's observer was irrevocably dark and opaque.[19]

Schopenhauer's importance here lies in the very modernity of the observer he describes, and at the same time in the ambiguity of that observer. Certainly Schopenhauer provides a crucial anticipatory statement of modernist aesthetics and art theory in his articulation of an autonomous artistic perception. This more familiar dimension of his work outlines the grounds for a detached observer with "visionary" capabilities, characterized by a subjectivism that no longer can be called Kantian. Yet it is crucial to affirm Scho-

18.　Arthur Schopenhauer, *The World As Will and Representation*, trans. E. F. J. Payne (New York, 1966), vol. 2, p. 22.
19.　Schopenhauer, *The World As Will and Representation*, vol. 2, p. 491.

penhauer's immediate adjacency to a scientific discourse about the human subject against which later proponents of an autonomous artistic vision supposedly rebelled. The arch anti-metaphysician Ernst Mach, in 1885, in fact credited both Goethe and Schopenhauer with founding a modern physiology of the senses.[20] In the following pages I want to suggest how Schopenhauer's complex interlacing of a scientific and an aesthetic discourse about vision is essential to an understanding of modernity and the observer, and how it challenges any simplistic opposition of nineteenth-century art and science as discrete and separate domains.

Although Schopenhauer termed his own philosophy "idealist" and conventional accounts have routinely identified him as a "subjective idealist," such labels misconstrue the heterogeneous texture of his thought. Never has an idealist been so immersed in the details of corporeality or alluded to such a large range of texts about human physiology, repeatedly situating his most central ideas in relation to the specific anatomy of the brain, the nervous system, and the spinal cord.[21] So often has Schopenhauer's aesthetics been detached or presented independently, that its fundamental affiliation with the supplements to *The World As Will and Representation* is forgotten. But his aesthetic subject, an observer freed from the demands of the will, of the body, capable of "pure perception," and of becoming "the clear eye of the world" is not separate from his preoccupation with the science of physiology.[22] The more Schopenhauer involved himself in the new collective knowledge of a fragmented body composed of separate organic systems, subject to the opacity of the sensory organs and dominated by involuntary reflex activity, the more intensely he sought to establish a visuality that escaped the demands of that body.

Although formed by Kant's aesthetics and epistemology in fundamental ways, Schopenhauer undertakes what he calls his "correction" of Kant: to

20.   Ernst Mach, *Contributions to the Analysis of the Sensations*, trans. C. M. Williams (La Salle, Ill., 1890), p. 1.
21.   Relatively little has been written on this dimension of Schopenhauer. See, for example, Maurice Mandelbaum, "The Physiological Orientation of Schopenhauer's Epistemology," in *Schopenhauer: His Philosophical Achievement*, ed. Michael Fox (Sussex, 1980), pp. 50–67, and Joachim Gerlach, "Über neurologische Erkenntniskritik," *Schopenhauer-Jahrbuch*, 53 (1972), pp. 393–401.
22.   Schopenhauer, *The World As Will and Representation*, vol. 2, pp. 367–371.

reverse Kant's privileging of abstract thinking over perceptual knowledge, and to insist on the physiological makeup of the subject as the site on which the formation of representations occurs.[23] Schopenhauer's answer to the Kantian problem of *Vorstellung* removes us completely from the classical terms of the camera obscura: "What is representation? A very complicated *physiological* occurence in an animal's brain, whose result is the consciousness of a *picture* or *image* at that very spot."[24] What Kant called the synthetic unity of apperception, Schopenhauer unhesitatingly identifies as the cerebrum of the human brain. Schopenhauer here is but one instance in the first half of the nineteenth century of what has been called "the physiological reinterpretation of the Kantian critique of reason."[25] "A philosophy like the Kantian, that ignores entirely [the physiological] point of view, is one-sided and therefore inadequate. It leaves an immense gulf between our philosophical and physiological knowledge, with which we can never be satisfied."[26]

For Theodor Adorno, Schopenhauer's distance from Kant is due in part to his recognition that the transcendental subject is mere illusion, "a phantom," and the only unity Schopenhauer can finally accord to the subject is biological.[27] Implicit in Adorno's remarks, however, is that once the phenomenal self is reduced to simply one empirical object among others, the autonomy and authenticity of its representations are also put in question. What haunts Schopenhauer's postulation of a noumenal realm of "entirely objective perception" is his simultaneous delineation of the observer as physiological apparatus adequate for the consumption of a preexisting world of "pictures" and "images." If at the core of all Schopenhauer's work is his aversion to the instinctual life of the body, to the ceaseless and monotonous repetition of its pulses and desires, his utopia of aesthetic perception was also a retreat from

23.   Schopenhauer, *The World As Will and Representation*, vol. 2, p. 273.
24.   Schopenhauer, *The World As Will and Representation*, vol. 2, p. 191. Emphasis in original.
25.   Herbert Schnädelbach, *Philosophy in Germany 1831–1933*, trans. Eric Matthews (Cambridge, 1984), p. 105. See also David E. Leary, "The Philosophical Development of Psychology in Germany 1780–1850," *Journal of the History of the Behavioral Sciences* 14, no. 2 (April 1978), pp. 113–121.
26.   Schopenhauer, *The World As Will and Representation*, vol. 2, p. 273.
27.   Theodor Adorno, *Minima Moralia*, trans. E. F. Jephcott (London, 1974), pp. 153–154.

the anguish of a modernized world that was making the body into an apparatus of predictable reflex activity, outlined by the scientists whose work so
fascinated him. And Nietzsche's critique of Schopenhauer's aesthetics insists
that his "pure perception" was fundamentally an escape from the sexual
body.[28]

In fact, Schopenhauer arrived at his definitive conflation of the subjective and the physiological during the long interval separating the first and second editions of *The World as Will and Representation,* between 1819 to 1844,
a period in Europe when the idea of both the optical apparatus and the human
body underwent profound transformation. Schopenhauer's expansion of his
text parallels the explosion of physiological research and publishing, and the
second edition records his extraordinary assimilation of large amounts of scientific material. For example, the figure of Xavier Bichat was of great importance to Schopenhauer.[29] Bichat's *Recherches physiologiques sur la vie et la
mort* (1800) is termed "one of the most profoundly conceived works in the
whole of French literature," and, Schopenhauer adds, "his reflections and
mine mutually support each other, since his are the physiological commentary on mine, and mine are the philosophical commentary on his; and we shall
best be understood by being read together side by side."[30] Although by the
1840s Bichat's work was generally considered scientifically obsolete and part
of an increasingly discredited vitalism, he nonetheless provided Schopenhauer with a crucial physical model of the human subject. Bichat's physiological conclusions grew primarily out of his study of death, in which he
identified death as a fragmented process, consisting of the extinction of different organs and processes: the death of locomotion, of respiration, of sense
perceptions, of the brain. If death was thus a multiple, dispersed event, then
so was organic life. According to Georges Canguilhem, "The genius of Bichat
was to decentralize the notion of life, to incarnate it in the parts of organ-

28.   Nietzsche, *Genealogy of Morals,* trans. Walter Kaufmann (New York, 1968), pp.
104–105.
29.   On Bichat see Elizabeth Haigh, *Xavier Bichat and the Medical Theory of the Eighteenth Century*, (London, 1984) esp. pp. 87–117, and Michel Foucault, *The Birth of the
Clinic,* trans. A. M. Sheridan Smith (New York, 1973), pp. 125–146. See also Paul Janet,
"Schopenhauer et la physiologie française: Cabanis et Bichat," *Revue des Deux Mondes* 39
(May 1880), pp. 35–59.
30.   Schopenhauer, *The World As Will and Representation,* vol. 2, p. 261.

isms."[31] With Bichat begins the progressive parcelization and division of the body into separate and specific systems and functions that would occur in the first half of the nineteenth century. One of these functions was, of course, the sense of sight.

The subjective vision affirmed by Goethe and Schopenhauer that endowed the observer with a new perceptual autonomy also coincided with the making of the observer into a subject of new knowledge and new techniques of power. The terrain on which these two interrelated observers emerged in the nineteenth century was the science of physiology. From 1820 into the 1840s physiology was very unlike the specialized science it later became; it had then no formal institutional identity and came into being as the accumulated work of disconnected individuals from diverse branches of learning.[32] In common was the excitement and wonderment about the body, which now appeared like a new continent to be explored, mapped, and mastered, with new recesses and mechanisms now uncovered for the first time. But the real importance of physiology has less to do with any empirical discoveries than that it became the arena for new types of epistemological reflection that depended on knowledge about the eye and processes of vision; it signals how the body was becoming the site of both power and truth. Physiology at this moment of the nineteenth century is one of those sciences that mark the rupture that Foucault poses between the eighteenth and nineteenth centuries, in which man emerges as a being in whom the transcendent is mapped onto the empirical.[33] It was the discovery that knowledge was conditioned by the physical and anatomical functioning of the body, and perhaps most importantly, of the eyes. Yet physiology, as a science of life, equally signals the appearance of new methods of power. "When the diagram of power abandons the model of sovereignty in favor of a disciplinary model, when it

31.   Georges Canguilhem, "Bichat et Bernard," *Etudes d'histoire et de philosophie des sciences* (Paris, 1983), p. 161. See Jean-Paul Sartre's characterization of nineteenth-century empiricism in *The Family Idiot: Gustave Flaubert 1821–1857* vol. 1, trans. Carol Cosman (Chicago, 1981), pp. 472–475: "The principles of empiricist ideology conceal an analytic intelligence . . . an active method organized to reduce a whole to its parts."
32.   On how new concepts of physiology were metaphorically transferred to the social sciences in the nineteenth century, see Paul Rabinow, *French Modern: Norms and Forms of the Social Environment* (Cambridge, Mass., 1989), pp. 25–26.
33.   Michel Foucault, *The Order of Things* (New York, 1971), pp. 318–320.

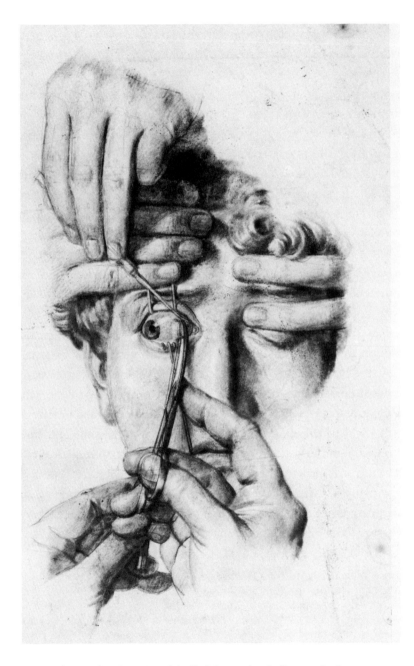

Drawing by Nicolas-Henri Jacob in Traité complet de l'anatomie de
l'homme *by Marc-Jean Bourgery. 1839.*

becomes the 'bio-power' or 'bio-politics' of populations, controlling and administering life, *it is indeed life that emerges as the new object of power.*"[34]

The collective achievement of European physiology in the first half of the nineteenth century was a comprehensive survey of a previously half-known territory, an exhaustive inventory of the body. It was a knowledge that also would be the basis for the formation of an individual adequate to the productive requirements of economic modernity and for emerging technologies of control and subjection. By the 1840s there had been both (1) the gradual transferral of the holistic study of subjective experience or mental life to an empirical and quantitative plane, and (2) the division and fragmentation of the physical subject into increasingly specific organic and mechanical systems. Bichat contributed to this decentralization by locating functions like memory and intelligence in the brain and situating the emotions in various internal organs. The work of Franz Joseph Gall (whose lectures Schopenhauer eagerly attended as a student) and Johann Gaspar Spurzheim located the mind and emotions exclusively in the brain. Spurzheim, for example, identified the sites of thirty-five brain functions. This kind of mental mapping differed from earlier efforts in that the localization was done by means of objective external induction and experiment, and no longer through subjective introspection.[35] By the early 1820s the work of Sir Charles Bell and François Magendie had articulated the morphological and functional distinction between sensory and motor nerves.[36] Johannes Müller, in 1826, improved on Bell and Magendie by determining that sensory nerves are of five types, further specializing the perceiving subject.[37] Also in the mid-1820s, Pierre Flourens announced the discovery of the functions of the different parts of the human brain, in particular the distinction between the cerebellum, the motor center, and the cerebrum,

34.   Gilles Deleuze, *Foucault*, p. 92. Emphasis added.
35.   See Jean-Pierre Changeux, *Neuronal Man: The Biology of Mind*, trans. Dr. Lawrence Garey (New York, 1985), p. 14. For further background, see Robert Young, *Mind, Brain, and Adaptation in the Nineteenth Century* (Oxford, 1970), pp. 54–101.
36.   See Oswei Temkin, "The Philosophical Background of Magendie's Physiology," *Bulletin of the History of Medicine* 20 (1946), pp. 10–27.
37.   Johannes Müller, *Zur Vergleichenden Physiologie des Gesichtssinnes des Menschen und der Thiere* (Leipzig, 1826), pp. 6–9.

a perception center.[38] All this research built up a certain "truth" of the body
that provided a ground for Schopenhauer's discourse on the subject.[39]

It was, in particular, Flourens's localization of motor activity and per-
ceptive activity, that is, a separation of sight and hearing from muscular movement, that provided Schopenhauer with a model for isolating aesthetic
perception from the systems responsible simply for the subsistence of the
body. In "common, ordinary man, that manufactured article of nature, which
she daily produces in thousands," vision was hardly differentiated from these
"lower" functions. But in artists and "men of genius," the sense of sight was
the highest ranked because of its "indifference with regard to the will," or in
other words its anatomical separation from the systems regulating mere
instinctual life. Flourens provided a physiological diagram that allowed a spa-
tialization of this hierarchy of functions. It is not difficult to see Schopenhauer's affiliation with later dualist theories of perception, for example in the
work of Konrad Fiedler (free artistic and unfree nonartistic perception), Alois
Riegl (haptic and optic perception), and Theodor Lipps (positive and negative
empathy)—all of which were then severed from the immediacy of the body
and were posed as dualist systems of transcendental modes of perception.[40]

Schopenhauer received additional confirmation from research on
reflex action, specifically from the work of the British physician Marshall Hall,
who in the early 1830s demonstrated how the spinal cord is responsible for
a number of bodily activities independently of the brain. Hall made a categorical distinction between voluntary "cerebral" activity of the nervous system

38.   Pierre Flourens, *Recherches expérimentales sur les propriétés et les fonctions du système nerveux dans les animaux vertébrés* (Paris, 1824), pp. 48–92.
39.   It should be remembered that the struggles in the early nineteenth century between
"localizationists" and "anti-localizationists" took on political significance. Proponents of
cerebral localization "were seen as regicidal, hostile to the status quo, against the death
penalty, for lowering property qualifications for the right to vote, denying the immortality
of the soul . . . anticlerical, atheist, even republican; the cerebral unitarians are legitimist."
Henri Hacaen and G. Lanteri-Laura, *Evolutions des connaissances et des doctrines sur les
localisations cérébrales* (Paris, 1977), p. 45.
40.   Wilhelm Worringer, for example, cites Schopenhauer in relation to the dualist aesthetics of Theodor Lipps, in *Abstraction and Empathy* [1908], trans. Michael Bullock (New
York, 1948), p. 137. The likely link between Schopenhauer's work and Riegl's "Kunst-
wollen" is briefly suggested by Otto Pacht in "Art Historians and Art Critics: Alois Riegl,"
Burlington Magazine (May 1963), pp. 188–193.

and involuntary "excito-motor" activity in a way that seemed to corroborate Schopenhauer's own distinction between mere stimulus or irritability and a notion of sensibility (derived from Kant).[41] Yet both of these higher and lower capacities were localities within the same biological organism. In the following passage Schopenhauer maps out, with startling explicitness, the embeddedness of aesthetic perception in the empirical edifice of the body:

> Now in the ascending series of animals, the nervous and muscular systems *separate* ever more distinctly from each other, till in the vertebrates, and most completely in man, the nervous system is divided into an organic and a cerebral nervous system. This cerebral nervous system, again, is developed to the extremely complicated apparatus of the cerebrum and cerebellum, the spinal cord, cerebral and spinal nerves, sensory and motor nerve fascicles. Of these only the cerebrum, together with the sensory nerves attached to it, and the posterior spinal nerve fascicles are intended to *take up* the motives from the external world. All the other parts, on the other hand, are intended only to *transmit* the motives to the muscles in which the will directly manifests itself. Bearing the above separation in mind, we see the *motive separated* to the same extent more and more distinctly *in consciousness* from the *act of will* it calls forth, as is the *representation* from the *will*. Now in this way the *objectivity* of consciousness is constantly increasing, since in it the representations exhibit themselves more and more distinctly and purely. . . . This is the point where the present consideration, starting from physiological foundations, is connected with the subject of our third book, the metaphysics of the beautiful.[42]

Within a single paragraph, we are swept from sensory nerve fascicles to the beautiful; or more broadly, from the sheer reflex functioning of the body to the will-less perception of "the pure eye of genius." The concept of art may

41. For Hall, "The cerebral system is volition, perception," while emotions and passions were located in what he called "true spinal marrow, (or system)." *Memoirs on the Nervous System* (London, 1837), pp. 70–71. See also Edwin Clarke and L. S. Jacyna, *Nineteenth Century Origins of Neuroscientific Concepts* (Berkeley, 1987), pp. 127–129.
42. Schopenhauer, *The World As Will and Representation*, vol. 2, pp. 290–291.

be absolute for Schopenhauer, but the possibility of his aesthetic perception is nonetheless grounded in the specificity of human corporeality described by contemporary empirical science. The possibility of "pure perception" is thus derived from the same accumulation of physiological knowledge that was simultaneously shaping a new productive and controllable human subject. Far from being a transcendental form of knowledge, this perception is a biological capacity, and one that is not uniform in all men or women:

> The sight of beautiful objects, a beautiful view for example, is also a phenomenon of the brain. Its purity and perfection depend not merely on the object, but also on the quality and constitution of the brain, that is on its form and size, the fineness of its texture, and the stimulation of its activity through the energy of the pulse of its brain arteries.[43]

Not only is the apprehension of beauty physiologically determined, but Schopenhauer goes on to insist that there are physical methods capable of producing or modifying certain modes of perception.

> The state required for pure objectivity of perception has in part permanent conditions in the perfection of the brain and of the physiological quality generally favorable to its activity; in part temporary conditions, in so far as this state is favored by everything that increases the attention and enhances the susceptibility of the cerebral nervous system . . . everything that furnishes brain activity with an unforced ascendancy by a calming down of the blood circulation.[44]

Schopenhauer is here proposing specific ways for "silencing the will" in order to bring about a state of "pure objectivity" and to "lose oneself in perception." Once it is understood that perception depends on the physical structure and functioning of an empirically constituted human organism *and* that there are techniques of the body or practical procedures for externally modifying perception, the claim of Schopenhauer's observer to autonomy becomes a wishful fiction. Schopenhauer's application of knowledge of the body to "increase

43.   Schopenhauer, *The World As Will and Representation*, vol. 2, p. 24.
44.   Schopenhauer, *The World As Will and Representation*, vol. 2, pp. 367–368.

the attention" in order to attain the "pure objectivity of perception" is a project whose *conditions of possibility* are essentially the same as those of the emerging physiological psychology of the nineteenth century. An important part of this new discipline was the quantitative study of the eye in terms of attentiveness, reaction times, thresholds of stimulation, and fatigue. Such studies were clearly related to the demand for knowledge about the adaptation of a human subject to productive tasks in which optimum attention was indispensable for the rationalization and making efficient of human labor. The economic need for rapid coordination of eye and hand in performing repetitive actions required precise knowledge of human optical and sensory capacities. In the context of new industrial models of production, the problem of "inattention" by workers was a serious one, with economic and disciplinary consequences.[45] Moreover, it should be stressed that Schopenhauer's aesthetics and contemporary quantitative psychological research, no matter how divergent their respective notions of "attention," are both constituted by the same discourse of the subject, in which the physiological is fully immanent to the subjective.[46] It is knowledge that simultaneously provided techniques for the external control and domination of the human subject *and* was the emancipating ground for notions of subjective vision within modernist art theory and experimentation. Any effective account of modern culture must confront the ways in which modernism, rather than being a reaction against or transcendence of processes of scientific and economic rationalization, is inseparable from them.

The physiological optics outlined by Goethe and Schopenhauer with their models of subjective vision (which was brought to fulfillment by Helmholtz

45.   See Didier Deleule and François Guéry, *Le corps productif* (Paris, 1972), pp. 85–86.
46.   The problem of "attention" became a central problem in the scientific psychology of the later nineteenth century, particularly in the work of Wilhelm Wundt. See Théodule Ribot, *La psychologie d'attention* (Paris, 1889), and Henri Bergson, *Matter and Memory* [1896], trans. N. M. Paul and W. S. Palmer (New York, 1988), pp. 99–104. Bergson asserts: "Stage by stage we shall be led to define attention as an adaptation of the body rather than of the mind," and, like Schopenhauer, insists that "the essential effect of attention is to render perception more intense." On the impact of these later notions of attention, see my "Spectacle, Attention, and Counter-memory," *October* 50 (Fall 1989), pp. 97–107.

in the 1860s) must be seen against the profound changes that took place in theories of the nature of light. The shift from emission and corpuscular theories to undulatory or wave-motion explanations have a major significance for nineteenth-century culture as a whole.[47] The wave theory of light made obsolete the notion of a rectilinear propagation of light rays on which classical optics and, in part, the science of perspective was based. All the modes of representation derived from Renaissance and later models of perspective no longer had the legitimation of a science of optics. The verisimilitude associated with perspectival construction obviously persisted into the nineteenth century, but it was severed from the scientific base that had once authorized it and it could no longer have the same meanings it had when either Aristotelian or Newtonian optics held sway. Dominant theories of vision, whether of Alberti, Kepler, Newton (Huygens is the obvious exception), all described in their own fashion how a beam of isolated light rays traversed an optical system, with each ray taking the shortest possible route to reach its destination.[48] The camera obscura is inextricably wedded to this point-to-point epistemological setup. At the same time it must be stressed how deeply theological was the notion that light was radiant (composed of rays) and emanative.

The work of Augustin Jean Fresnel has come to stand for the paradigm shift.[49] By 1821 Fresnel had concluded that the vibrations of which light consisted were entirely *transverse*, which led him and subsequent researchers to build mechanical models of an ether that transmitted transverse waves rather than longitudinal rays or waves. Fresnel's work participates in the destruction

47.   See Jed Z. Buchwald, *The Rise of the Wave Theory of Light: Optical Theory and Experiment in the Early Nineteenth Century* (Chicago, 1989). See also P. M. Harman, *Energy, Force, and Matter: The Conceptual Development of Nineteenth-Century Physics* (Cambridge, 1982), pp. 19–26; Thomas S. Kuhn, *The Structure of Scientific Revolutions*, 2nd ed. (Chicago, 1970), pp. 73–74.
48.   For important background and bibliographical data see David C. Lindberg, *Theories of Vision from Al-Kindi to Kepler* (Chicago, 1976), and Gérard Simon, *Le regard, l'être et l'apparence dans l'optique de l'antiquité* (Paris, 1988).
49.   See Edward Frankel, "Corpuscular Optics and the Wave Theory of Light: The Science and Politics of a Revolution in Physics," *Social Studies of Science* 6 (1976), pp. 141–184; G. N. Cantor, *Optics After Newton* (Manchester, 1983), esp. pp. 150–159; and R. H. Silliman, "Fresnel and the Emergence of Physics as a Discipline," *Historical Studies in the Physical Sciences* 4 (1974), pp. 137–162.

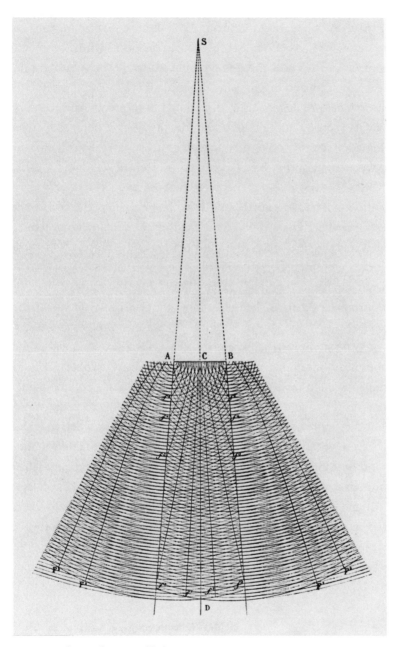

A.-J. Fresnel. Interference of light waves.

of classical mechanics, clearing the ground for the eventual dominance of modern physics. What had been a discrete domain of optics in the seventeenth and eighteenth centuries now merged with the study of other physical phenomena, i.e., electricity and magnetism. Above all, it is a moment when light loses its ontological privilege; and in the course of the nineteenth century, from Faraday to Maxwell, the independent identity of light became increasingly problematic. Goethe's color theory, with its proposal of a qualitative difference between light and color, had hinted at such developments. More importantly here, however, as light began to be conceived as an electromagnetic phenomenon it had less and less to do with the realm of the visible and with the description of human vision. So it is at this moment in the early nineteenth century that physical optics (the study of light and the forms of its propagation) merges with physics, and physiological optics (the study of the eye and its sensory capacities) suddenly came to dominate the study of vision.

An important landmark in the field of physiological optics and in the formation of a new observer was the publication of Johannes Müller's *Handbuch der Physiologie des Menschen*, beginning in 1833.[50] A massive summary of current physiological discourse, Müller's work presented a notion of the observer radically alien from that of the eighteenth century. Schopenhauer knew its contents well and it was a decisive influence on Müller's younger colleague Helmholtz. In thousands of sprawling pages Müller unfolded an image of the body as a multifarious factory-like enterprise, comprised of diversified processes and activities, run by measurable amounts of energy and labor. Ironically, this was one of the last influential texts to argue the case of vitalism, yet it also contained the very empirical information that was to finally extinguish vitalism as an acceptable idea. In his exhaustive analysis of the body into an array of physical and mechanical systems, Müller reduced the phenomenon of life to a set of physiochemical processes that were observable and manipulable in the laboratory. The idea of an organism becomes equivalent to an

---

50.   For publication and translation history see Edwin G. Boring, *A History of Experimental Psychology*, 2nd ed. (New York, 1957), p. 46. On Müller see Gottfried Köller, *Das Leben des Biologen Johannes Müller* (Stuttgart, 1958). Müller is called "the most outstanding, versatile, and respected medical scientist of the first half of the nineteenth century" in Clarke and Jayna, *Nineteenth Century Origins of Neuroscientific Concepts*, p. 25.

amalgamation of adjacent apparatuses. The distinction that Bichat had tried to maintain between the organic and the inorganic collapses under the sheer weight of Müller's inventory of the mechanical capacities of the body. The work was quickly to become the basis for the dominant work in mid-nineteenth-century psychology and physiology. It was to be particularly important for his pupil Helmholtz in the latter's description of the functioning of the human organism as fundamentally the manifestation of a certain quantity of power required to perform work.[51]

The most influential part of Müller's work was his study of the physiology of the senses, and his treatment of the sense of sight was by far the longest in this section of the work.[52] Although preceded by the work of Bell and Magendie, Müller made the most widely known statement of the subdivision and specialization of the human sensory apparatus. His fame came to rest on his theorization of that specialization: the doctrine of specific nerve energies (*spezifische Sinnesenergien*) introduced in the *Physiologie*. It was a theory in many ways as important in the nineteenth century as the Molyneux problem was in the eighteenth century. It was the acknowledged foundation of Helmholtz's *Optics*, which dominated the second half of the 1800s; in science, philosophy, and psychology it was widely propounded, debated, and denounced even into the early twentieth century.[53] In short, this was one of the most influential ways in which an observer was figured in the nineteenth century, a way in which a certain "truth" about sight and cognition was depicted.

The theory was based on the discovery that the nerves of the different senses were physiologically distinct, that is, capable of one determinant kind

51. One should note the pedagogical lineage: Müller was a teacher of Helmholtz who was a teacher of Ivan Sechenov who was a teacher of Ivan Pavlov.
52. Müller had already written two influential books on vision. See his *Zur vergleichenden Physiologie des Gesichtsinnes des Menschen und Thiere* (Leipzig, 1826), and *Über die phantastischen Gesichterscheinungen* (Coblenz, 1826).
53. For an important critique of the theory, see Henri Bergson, *Matter and Memory*, trans. N. M. Paul and W. S. Palmer (New York, 1988), pp. 50–54. Other assessments include Emile Meyerson, *Identity and Reality*, trans. Kate Loewenberg (New York, 1962), pp. 292–293, and Moritz Schlick, "Notes and Commentary," *Boston Studies in the Philosophy of Science* 37 (1974), p. 165. See also William R. Woodward, "Hermann Lotze's Critique of Johannes Müller's Doctrine of Specific Sense," *Medical History* vol. 19, no. 2 (April 1975), pp. 147–157.

of sensation only, and not of those proper to the other organs of sense.[54] It asserted quite simply—and this is what marks its epistemological scandal—that a uniform cause (for example, electricity) generates utterly different sensations from one kind of nerve to another. Electricity applied to the optic nerve produces the experience of light, applied to the skin the sensation of touch. Conversely, Müller showed that a variety of different causes will produce the *same* sensation in a given sensory nerve. In other words, he is describing a fundamentally arbitrary relation between stimulus and sensation. It is an account of a body with an innate capacity, one might even say a transcendental faculty, to *misperceive*—of an eye that renders differences equivalent.

His most exhaustive demonstration here is with the sense of sight, and he arrives at the astonishing conclusion that the observer's experience of light has no necessary connection with any actual light.[55] In fact, his chapter on vision is subtitled "Physical Conditions Necessary for the Production of Luminous Images," a phrase that would have been unimaginable before the nineteenth century. He then proceeds to enumerate the agencies capable of producing the sensation of light:

> 1. By the undulations or emanations which from their action on the eye are called light, although they may have many other actions than this; for instance, they effect chemical changes, and are the means of maintaining the organic processes in plants.
>
> 2. By mechanical influences; as concussion or a blow.
>
> 3. By electricity.

54.   His opening premises are the following:

> 1. The same internal cause excites in the different senses different sensations and in each sense the sensations peculiar to it.
> 2. The same external cause also gives rise to different sensations in each sense according to the special endowments of the nerve.
> 3. The peculiar sensation of each nerve can be excited by several distinct causes, internal and external.

Elements of Physiology, vol. 2, p. 1061.

55.   Sir Charles Eastlake, in the notes to his 1840 translation of Goethe's *Theory of Colours*, cites Müller as demonstrating "the inherent capacity of the organ of vision to produce light and colours" (p. 373).

4. By chemical agents, such as narcotics, digitalis, &c. which, being absorbed into the blood, give rise to the appearance of luminous sparks, &c. before the eyes independently of any external cause.

5. By the stimulus of the blood in a state of congestion. (1064)

Further on Müller reiterates these possibilities: "The sensations of light and color are produced wherever aliquot parts of the retina are excited by any internal stimulus such as the blood, or by an external stimulus such as mechanical pressure, electricity, &c." The "&c." seems added almost begrudgingly as Müller concedes that radiant light, too, can produce "luminous images."

Again the camera obscura model is made irrelevant. The experience of light becomes severed from any stable point of reference or from any source or origin around which a world could be constituted and apprehended. Sight here has been specialized and separated certainly, but it no longer resembles any classical models. The theory of specific nerve energies presents the outlines of a visual modernity in which the "referential illusion" is unsparingly laid bare. The very absence of referentiality is the ground on which new instrumental techniques will construct for an observer a new "real" world. It is a question, in the early 1830s, of a perceiver whose very empirical nature renders identities unstable and mobile, and for whom sensations are interchangeable. In effect, vision is redefined as a capacity for being affected by sensations that have no necessary link to a referent, thus imperiling any coherent system of meaning. Müller's theory was potentially so nihilistic that it is no wonder Helmholtz, Hermann Lotze, and others, who accepted its empirical premises, were impelled to invent theories of cognition and signification that concealed its uncompromising cultural implications. Helmholtz put forward his celebrated notion of "unconscious inference" and Lotze his theory of "local signs." Both wanted an epistemology based on subjective vision, but one that guaranteed dependable knowledge without the threat of arbitrariness.[56] What was at stake and seemed so threatening was not just a new form

56.   Helmholtz attempted to establish regular but nonmimetic relations between sensations and external objects and events. See his *Handbook of Physiological Optics*, vol. 2, New York, Dover, 1962, pp. 10–35. But later, Helmholtz's "psychologism" was to become the target of neo-Kantians who sought to reestablish a ground for a priori knowledge.

of epistemological skepticism about the unreliability of the senses, but a positive reorganization of perception and its objects. The issue was not just how does one know what is real, but that new forms of the real were being fabricated, and a new truth about the capacities of a human subject was being articulated in these terms.

Müller's theory eradicated distinctions between internal and external sensation, which were implicitly preserved in the work of Goethe and Schopenhauer as notions of "inner light" or "inner vision." Now, however, interiority is drained of any meaning that it had for a classical observer, or for the model of the camera obscura, and all sensory experience occurs on a single immanent plane. The subject outlined in his *Physiologie* is homologous with the contemporary phenomenon of photography: an essential property of both is the action of physical and chemical agents on a sensitized surface. But in his supposedly empirical description of the human sensory apparatus, Müller presents not a unitary subject but a composite structure on which a wide range of techniques and forces could produce or simulate manifold experiences that are all equally "reality." Thus the idea of subjective vision here has less to do with a post-Kantian subject who is "the organizer of the spectacle in which he appears," than it does with a process of subjectivization in which the subject is simultaneously the object of knowledge and the object of procedures of control and normalization.

When Müller distinguishes the human eye from the compound eyes of crustacea and insects, he seems to be citing our optical equipment as a kind of Kantian faculty that organizes sensory experience in a necessary and unchanging way. But his work, in spite of his praise of Kant, implies something quite different. Far from being apodictic or universal in nature, like the "spectacles" of time and space, our physiological apparatus is again and again shown to be defective, inconsistent, prey to illusion, and, in a crucial manner, susceptible to external procedures of manipulation and stimulation that have the essential capacity *to produce experience for the subject*. Ironically, the notions of the reflex arc and reflex action, which in the seventeenth century referred to vision and the optics of reflection, begin to become the centerpiece of an emerging technology of the subject, culminating in the work of Pavlov.

In his account of the relation between stimulus and sensation, Müller suggests not an orderly and legislative functioning of the senses, but rather their receptivity to calculated management and derangement. Emil Dubois-Reymond, the colleague of Helmholtz, seriously pursued the possibility of electrically cross-connecting nerves, enabling the eye to see sounds and the ear to hear colors, well before Rimbaud's celebration of sensory dislocation. It should be emphasized that Müller's research, and that of the psychophysicists who follow him in the nineteenth century, is inseparable from the technical and conceptual resources made available by contemporary work in electricity and chemistry. Some of the empirical evidence presented by Müller had been available since antiquity or was in the domain of common-sense knowledge.[57] What is new, however, is the extraordinary privilege given to a complex of electrophysical techniques. What constitutes "sensation" is dramatically expanded and transformed, and it has little in common with how sensation was discussed in the eighteenth century. The adjacency of Müller's doctrine of specific nerve energies to the technology of nineteenth-century modernity is made particularly clear by Helmholtz:

> Nerves have been often and not unsuitably compared to telegraph wires. Such a wire conducts one kind of electric current and no other; it may be stronger, it may be weaker, it may move in either direction; it has no other qualitative differences. Nevertheless, according to the different kinds of apparatus with which we provide its terminations, we can send telegraphic dispatches, ring bells, explode mines, decompose water, move magnets, magnetize iron, develop light, and so on. *So with the nerves.* The condition of excitement which can be produced in them, and is conducted by them, is . . . everywhere the same.[58]

57.   Within a very different intellectual context, Thomas Hobbes presented some of the same basic evidence as Müller's: "And as pressing, rubbing, or striking the eye, makes us fancy a light; and pressing the ear, produceth a din; so do the bodies also we see, or hear, produce the same by their strong, though unobserved action." *Leviathan* [1651]. ed. Michael Oakeshott (Oxford, 1957), p. 8.

58.   Hermann von Helmholtz, *On the Sensations of Tone*, trans. Alexander Ellis, 2nd English ed. (1863; New York, 1954), pp. 148–149 (emphasis added). On other nineteenth-

Far from the specialization of the senses, Helmholtz is explicit about the body's indifference to the sources of its experience and of its capacity for multiple connections with other agencies and machines. The perceiver here becomes a neutral conduit, one kind of relay among others allowing optimum conditions of circulation and exchangeability, whether it be of commodities, energy, capital, images, or information.

Thus a neat homology between Müller's separation of the senses and the division of labor in the nineteenth century is not fully supportable. Even for Marx, the historical separation and increasing specification of the senses were, on the contrary, conditions for a modernity in which a fullness of human productive powers would be realized.[59] The problem for Marx under capitalism was not the separation of the senses but rather their estrangement by property relations; vision, for example, had been reduced to the sheer "sense of *having*." In what may be seen as a kind of reformulation of Müller's theory of specific nerve energies, Marx, in 1844, foresees an emancipated social world in which the differentiation and autonomy of the senses will be even more heightened: "To the *eye* an object comes to be other than it is to the *ear*, and the object of the eye is another object than the object of the ear. The specific character of each essential power is precisely its *specific essence*, and therefore also the specific mode of its objectification."[60] This is Marx sounding like a modernist, postulating a utopia of disinterested perception, a world devoid of exchange values in which vision can revel in its own pure operation. It was also in the 1840s that John Ruskin began to articulate his own notion of a specialized, heightened vision, and like Marx he implies that the separation and specialization of the senses is not the same as the fragmentation of human labor. By the 1850s Ruskin, in a celebrated passage, is able to define the capacities of a new kind of observer:

---

century analogies between nerves and telegraphy, see Dolf Sternberger, *Panorama of the Nineteenth Century*, pp. 34–37.

59.   See Karl Marx, *Economic and Philosophic Manuscripts of 1844*, trans. Martin Milligan (New York, 1968), pp. 139–141: "The forming of the five senses is a labor of the entire history of the world down to the present." See the related discussion in Fredric Jameson, *The Political Unconscious* (Ithaca, 1981), pp. 62–64.

60.   Marx, *Economic and Philosophic Manuscripts of 1844*, p. 140. Emphasis in original.

> The whole technical power of painting depends on our recovery
> of what may be called the *innocence of the eye*; that is to say, of a
> sort of childish perception of these flat stains of colour, merely as
> such, without consciousness of what they signify,—as a blind man
> would see them if suddenly gifted with sight.[61]

Clearly Ruskin is affirming a kind of primal opticality that was not even a possibility amid the eighteenth-century responses to the Molyneux problem. But it is more important to see that Ruskin and Müller are both modernizing vision in the same way, that a mapping out of an "innocent" vision is common to both. Ruskin's own starting point in describing the specific character of vision is actually much the same as that of Helmholtz. Compare Ruskin in *The Elements of Drawing*, "Everything that you can see in the world around you presents itself to your eyes only as an arrangement of patches of different colours variously shaded," with Helmholtz, "Everything our eye sees it sees as an aggregate of coloured surfaces in the visual field—that is its form of visual intuition."[62] Decades before related utterances by Maurice Denis, Alois Riegl, and others, Helmholtz used this premise for constructing a normalized and quantifiable model of human vision. Yet Ruskin was equally able to employ it in suggesting the possibility of a purified subjective vision, of an immediate and unfiltered access to the evidence of this privileged sense. But if the vision of Ruskin, Cézanne, Monet, and others has anything in common, it would be

61.   John Ruskin, *The Works of John Ruskin*, vol. 15, p. 27. For an important discussion of Ruskin's "innocent eye," see Phillipe Junod, *Transparence et opacité: Essai sur les fondements théoriques de l'art moderne* (Lausanne, 1975), pp. 159–170. See also Paul de Man, "Literary History and Literary Modernity," in *Blindness and Insight: Essays in the Rhetoric of Contemporary Criticism* (New York, 1971), pp. 142–165: "Modernity exists in the form of a desire to wipe out whatever came earlier, in the hope of reaching at last a point that could be called a true present, a point of origin that marks a new departure. This combined interplay of deliberate forgetting with an action that is also a new origin reaches the full power of the idea of modernity. . . . The human figures that epitomize modernity are defined by experiences such as childhood or convalescence, a freshness of perception that results from a slate wiped clear, from the absence of a past that has not yet had time to tarnish the immediacy of perception (although what is thus freshly discovered prefigures the end of this very freshness)."
62.   John Ruskin, *The Works of John Ruskin*, ed. E. T. Cook and Alexander Wedderburn (London, 1903–12), vol. 15, p. 27; Hermann von Helmholtz, "The Facts in Perception," *Popular Scientific Lectures* (London, 1885), p. 86.

misleading to call it "innocence." Rather it is a question of a vision achieved at great cost that claimed for the eye a vantage point uncluttered by the weight of historical codes and conventions of seeing, a position from which vision can function without the imperative of composing its contents into a reified "real" world.[63] It was a question of an eye that sought to avoid the repetitiveness of the formulaic and conventional, even as the effort time and again to see afresh and anew entailed its own pattern of repetition and conventions. And thus the "pure perception," the sheer optical attentiveness of modernism increasingly had to exclude or submerge that which would obstruct its functioning: language, historical memory, and sexuality.

But Müller and other researchers had already demonstrated a form of "pure" perception, by reducing the eye to its most elemental capacities, by testing the limits of its receptivity, and by liberating sensation from signification. If Ruskin, and other important figures in later visual modernism, sought an "infantine" obliviousness to signification, the empirical sciences of the 1830s and 1840s had begun to describe a comparable neutrality of the observer that was a precondition for the external mastery and annexing of the body's capacities, for the perfection of technologies of attention, in which sequences of stimuli or images can produce the same effect repeatedly as if for the first time. The achievement then of that kind of optical neutrality, the reduction of the observer to a supposedly rudimentary state, was both an aim of artistic experimentation of the second half of the nineteenth century *and* a condition for the formation of an observer who would be competent to consume the vast new amounts of visual imagery and information increasingly circulated during this same period. It was the remaking of the visual field not into a tabula rasa on which orderly representations could be arrayed, but into a surface of inscription on which a promiscuous range of effects could be produced. The visual culture of modernity would coincide with such techniques of the observer.

63.   See T. J. Clark, *The Painting of Modern Life*, p. 17. "In Cézanne, we could say, painting took the ideology of the visual—the notion of seeing as a separate activity with its own truth, its own particular access to the thing-in-itself—to its limits and breaking point."

Our eye finds it more comfortable to respond to a given stimulus by reproducing once more an image that it has produced many times before, instead of registering what is different and new in an impression.

—Friedrich Nietzsche

The retinal afterimage is perhaps the most important optical phenomenon discussed by Goethe in his chapter on physiological colors in the *Theory of Colours*. Though preceded by others in the late eighteenth century, his treatment of the topic was by far the most thorough up to that moment.[1] Subjective visual phenomena such as afterimages had been recorded since antiquity but only as events outside the domain of optics and they were relegated to the category of the "spectral" or mere appearance. But in the early nineteenth century, particularly with Goethe, such experiences attain the status of optical "truth." They are no longer deceptions that obscure a "true" perception; rather they begin to constitute an irreducible component of human vision. For Goethe and the physiologists who followed him there was

1.   Goethe identifies some of these earlier researchers, including Robert W. Darwin (1766–1848), the father of Charles, and the French naturalist Buffon (1707–1788). See *Theory of Colours,* trans. Charles Eastlake (Cambridge, Mass., 1970), p. 1–2. See also Boring, *A History of Experimental Psychology* (New York, 1950), pp. 102–104.

no such thing as optical illusion: whatever the healthy corporal eye experienced was in fact optical truth.

The implications of the new "objectivity" accorded to subjective phenomena are several. First, as discussed in the previous chapter, the privileging of the afterimage allowed one to conceive of sensory perception as cut from any necessary link with an external referent. The afterimage—the presence of sensation in the absence of a stimulus—and its subsequent modulations posed a theoretical and empirical demonstration of autonomous vision, of an optical experience that was produced by and within the subject. Second, and equally important, is the introduction of temporality as an inescapable component of observation. Most of the phenomena described by Goethe in the *Theory of Colours* involve an unfolding over time: "The edge begins to be blue . . . the blue gradually encroaches inward . . . the image then becomes gradually fainter."[2] The virtual instantaneity of optical transmission (whether intromission or extromission) was an unquestioned foundation of classical optics and theories of perception from Aristotle to Locke. And the simultaneity of the camera obscura image with its exterior object was never questioned.[3] But as observation is increasingly tied to the body in the early nineteenth century, temporality and vision become inseparable. The shifting processes of one's own subjectivity experienced in time became synonymous with the act of seeing, dissolving the Cartesian ideal of an observer completely focused on an object.

But the problem of the afterimage and the temporality of subjective vision is lodged within larger epistemological issues in the nineteenth century. On one hand the attention given to the afterimage by Goethe and others parallels contemporary philosophical discourses that describe perception and cognition as essentially temporal processes dependent upon a dynamic amalgamation of past and present. Schelling, for example, describes a vision founded on just such a temporal overlapping:

2. Goethe, *Theory of Colours*, pp. 16–17. Nineteenth century science suggested "the idea of a reality which endures inwardly, which is duration itself." Henri Bergson, *Creative Evolution*, trans. Arthur Mitchell (New York, 1944), p. 395.
3. On the instantaneity of perception see, for example, David C. Lindberg, *Theories of Vision from Al-Kindi to Kepler* (Chicago, 1976), pp. 93–94.

> We do not live in vision; our knowledge is piecework, that is, it
> must be produced piece by piece in a fragmentary way, with divi-
> sions and gradations. . . . In the external world everyone sees more
> or less the same thing, and yet not everyone can express it. In order
> to complete itself, each thing runs through certain moments—*a*
> *series of processes following one another, in which the later always*
> *involves the earlier*, brings each thing to maturity.[4]

Earlier, in the preface to his *Phenomenology* (1807), Hegel makes a sweeping
repudiation of Lockean perception and situates perception within an unfolding that is temporal and historical. While attacking the apparent certainty of
sense perception, Hegel implicitly refutes the model of the camera obscura.
"It must be pointed out that truth is not like stamped coin issued ready from
the mint, and so can be taken up and used."[5] Although referring to the Lockean
notion of ideas "imprinting" themselves on passive minds, Hegel's remark has
a precocious applicability to photography, which, like coinage, offered
another mechanically and mass-produced form of exchangeable "truth."
Hegel's dynamic, dialectical account of perception, in which appearance
negates itself to become something other, finds an echo in Goethe's discussion of afterimages:

> The eye cannot for a moment remain in a particular state deter-
> mined by the object it looks upon. On the contrary, it is forced to
> a sort of opposition, which, in contrasting extreme with extreme,
> intermediate degree with intermediate degree, at the same time
> combines these opposite impressions, and thus ever tends to be
> whole, whether the impressions are successive or simultaneous
> and confined to one image.[6]

4.   F. W. J. Schelling, *The Ages of the World* [1815], trans. Fredrick de Wolfe Bolman (New
York, 1942), pp. 88–89. Emphasis added.
5.   G. W. F. Hegel, *The Phenomenology of Mind,* trans. J. B. Baillie (New York, 1967),
p. 98.
6.   Goethe, *Theory of Colours,* p. 13.

Goethe and Hegel, each in his own way, pose observation as the play and inter-action of forces and relations, rather than as the orderly contiguity of discrete stable sensations conceived by Locke or Condillac.[7]

Other writers of the time also delineated perception as a continuous process, a flux of temporally dispersed contents. The physicist André-Marie Ampère in his epistemological writings used the term *concrétion* to describe how any perception always blends with a preceding or remembered percep-tion. The words *mélange* and *fusion* occur frequently in his attack on classical notions of "pure" isolated sensations. Perception, as he wrote to his friend Maine de Biran, was fundamentally, "une suite de différences successives."[8] The dynamics of the afterimage are also implied in the work of Johann Fried-rich Herbart, who undertook one of the earliest attempts to quantify the move-ment of cognitive experience. Although his ostensible aim was to demonstrate and preserve Kant's notion of the unity of the mind, Herbart's formulation of mathematical laws governing mental experience in fact make him "a spiritual father of stimulus-response psychology."[9] If Kant gave a positive account of the mind's capacity for synthesizing and ordering experience, Herbart (Kant's successor at Königsberg) detailed how the subject wards off and prevents internal incoherence and disorganization. Consciousness, for Herbart, begins as a stream of potentially chaotic input from without. Ideas of things and events in the world were never copies of external reality but rather the out-come of an interactional process within the subject in which ideas (*Vorstel-lungen*) underwent operations of fusion, fading, inhibition, and blending

---

7.   It should be noted, however, that Hegel, in an 1807 letter to Schelling, criticized Goethe's color theory for being "restricted completely to the empirical." *Briefe von und an Hegel,* vol. 1, ed. Karl Hegel (Leipzig, 1884), p. 94. Cited in Karl Löwith, *From Hegel to Nietzsche: The Revolution in Nineteenth-Century Thought,* trans. David E. Green (New York, 1964), p. 13.

8.   André-Marie Ampère, "Lettre à Maine de Biran" [1809], in *Philosophie des Deux Ampères,* ed. J. Barthélemy-Saint-Hilaire (Paris, 1866), p. 236.

9.   Benjamin B. Wolman, "The Historical Role of Johann Friedrich Herbart," in *Histor-ical Roots of Contemporary Psychology,* ed. Benjamin B. Wolman (New York, 1968), p. 33. See also David E. Leary, "The Historical Foundations of Herbart's Mathematization of Psy-chology," *Journal of the History of the Behavioral Sciences* 16 (1980), pp. 150–163. For Her-bart's influence on later art theory and aesthetics see Michael Podro, *The Manifold in Perception: Theories of Art from Kant to Hildebrand* (Oxford, 1972); and Arturo Quinta-valle, "The Philosophical Context of Riegl's 'Stilfragen,'" in *On the Methodology of Archi-tectural History,* ed. Demetri Porphyrios (London, 1981), pp. 17–20.

(*Verschmelzungen*) with other previous or simultaneously occurring ideas or "presentations." The mind does not reflect truth but rather extracts it from an ongoing process involving the collision and merging of ideas.

> Let a series a, b, c, d, be given by perception; then, from the first movement of the perception and during its continuance, *a* is exposed to an arrest from other concepts already in consciousness. In the meantime, *a,* already partially sunken in consciousness, became more and more obscured when *b* came to it. This *b* at first unobscured, blended with the sinking *a*; then followed *c,* which itself unobscured, fused with *b,* which was becoming obscured. Similarly followed *d,* to become fused with *a, b,* and *c,* in different degrees. From this arises a law for each of these concepts. . . . It is very important to determine by calculation the degree of strength which a concept must attain in order to be able to stand beside two or more stronger ones exactly on the threshold of consciousness.[10]

All the processes of blending and opposition that Goethe described phenomenally in terms of the afterimage are for Herbart statable in differential equations and theorems. He specifically discusses color perception to describe the mental mechanisms of opposition and inhibition.[11] Once the operations of cognition become fundamentally measurable in terms of duration and intensity, it is thereby rendered both predictable and controllable. Although Herbart was philosophically opposed to empirical experimentation or any physiological research, his convoluted attempts to mathematize perception were important for the later quantitative sensory work of Müller, Gustav Fechner, Ernst Weber, and Wilhelm Wundt.[12] He was one of the first to recognize the potential crisis of meaning and representation implied by an autonomous subjectivity, and to propose a framework for its regimentation. Herbart clearly was attempting a quantification of *cognition,* but it nonetheless prepared the ground for attempts to measure the magnitude of sensations, and such mea-

10.   Johann Friedrich Herbart, *A Textbook in Psychology: An Attempt to Found the Science of Psychology on Experience, Metaphysics and Mathematics,* trans. Margaret K. Smith (New York, 1891), pp. 21–22.

11.   See Herbart, *Psychologie als Wissenschaft,* vol. 1 (Königsberg, 1824), pp. 222–224.

12.   For Herbart's influence on Müller, see the latter's *Elements of Physiology,* vol. 2, pp. 1380–1385.

surements required sensory experience that was durational. The afterimage was to become a crucial means by which observation could be quantified, by which the intensity and duration of retinal stimulation could be measured.

Also it is important to remember that Herbart's work was not simply abstract epistemological speculation but was directly tied to his pedagogical theories, which were influential in Germany and elsewhere in Europe during the mid-nineteenth century.[13] Herbart believed that his attempts to quantify psychological processes held the possibility for controlling and determining the sequential input of ideas into young minds, and in particular had the potential of instilling disciplinary and moral ideas. Obedience and attentiveness were central goals of Herbart's pedagogy. Just as new forms of factory production demanded more precise knowledge of a worker's attention span, so the management of the classroom, another disciplinary institution, demanded similar information.[14] In both cases the subject in question was measurable and regulated in time.

By the 1820s the quantitative study of afterimages was occurring in a wide range of scientific research throughout Europe. Working in Germany, the Czech Jan Purkinje continued Goethe's work on the persistence and modulation of afterimages: how long they lasted, what changes they went through, and under what conditions.[15] His empirical research and Herbart's mathematical methods were to come together in the next generation of psychologists and psychophysicists, when the threshold between the physiological and the mental became one of the primary objects of scientific practice. Instead of recording afterimages in terms of the lived time of the body as Goethe had generally done, Purkinje was the first to study them as part of a comprehensive

13.   For Herbart's theories of education, see Harold B. Dunkel, *Herbart and Herbartism: An Educational Ghost Story* (Chicago, 1970), esp. pp. 63–96.

14.   See Nikolas Rose, "The Psychological Complex: Mental Measurement and Social Administration," *Ideology and Consciousness* 5 (Spring 1979), pp. 5–70; and Didier Deleule and François Guéry, *Le corps productif* (Paris: 1973), pp. 72–89.

15   Purkinje wrote in Latin, which was translated by others into Czech. For relevant English translations, see "Visual Phenomena" [1823], trans. H. R. John, in William S. Sahakian, *History of Psychology: A Source Book in Systematic Psychology* (Itasca, Ill., 1968), pp. 101–108; and "Contributions to a Physiology of Vision," trans. Charles Wheatstone, *Journal of the Royal Institution* 1 (1830), pp. 101–117, reprinted in *Brewster and Wheatstone on Vision,* ed. Nicholas Wade (London, 1983), pp. 248–262.

Jan Purkinje. Afterimages. 1823.

quantification of the irritability of the eye.[16] He provided the first formal classification of different types of afterimages, and his drawings of them are a striking indication of the paradoxical objectivity of the phenomena of subjective
vision. Were we able to see the original drawings in color, we would have a
more vivid sense of their unprecedented overlapping of the visionary and the
empirical, of "the real" and the abstract.

Although working with relatively imprecise instruments, Purkinje timed
how long it took the eye to become fatigued, how long dilation and contrac-
tion of the pupil took, and measured the strength of eye movements. For Purkinje the physical surface of the eye itself became a field of statistical
information: he demarcated the retina in terms of how color changes hue
depending on where it strikes the eye, describing the extent of the area of visibility, quantified the distinction between direct and indirect vision, and also
gave a highly precise account of the blind spot.[17] The discourse of dioptrics,
of the transparency of refractive systems in the seventeenth and eighteenth
centuries, has given way to a mapping of the eye as a productive territory with
varying zones of efficiency and aptitude.

Beginning in the mid-1820s, the experimental study of afterimages led
to the invention of a number of related optical devices and techniques. Initially they were for purposes of scientific observation but were quickly con-
verted into forms of popular entertainment. Linking them all was the notion
that perception was not instantaneous, and the notion of a disjunction
between eye and object. Research on afterimages had suggested that some
form of blending or fusion occurred when sensations were perceived in quick

16.   Goethe provides a telling account of the subjectivity of the afterimage in which the
physiology of the attentive male eye and its functioning are inseparable from memory and
desire: "I had entered an inn towards evening, and, as a well favoured girl, with a brilliantly
fair complexion, black hair, and a scarlet bodice, came into the room, I looked attentively
at her as she stood before me at some distance in half shadow. As she presently afterwards
turned away, I saw on the white wall, which was now before me, a black face surrounded
with a bright light, while the dress of the perfectly distinct figure appeared of a beautiful
sea green." *Theory of Colours,* p. 22.
17.   It should be noted that Purkinje, in 1823, was the first scientist to formulate a classification system for fingerprints, another technique of producing and regulating human
subjects. See Vlasilav Krutz, "Purkinje, Jan Evangelista," *Dictionary of Scientific Biography*
vol. 11 (New York, 1975), pp. 213–217.

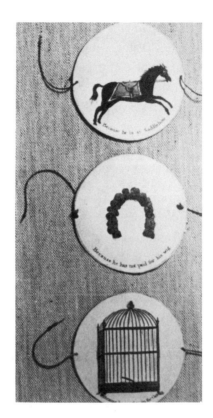

Thaumatropes. c. 1825.

succession, and thus the duration involved in seeing allowed its modification and control.

One of the earliest was the thaumatrope (literally, "wonder-turner"), first popularized in London by Dr. John Paris in 1825. It was a small circular disc with a drawing on either side and strings attached so that it could be twirled with a spin of the hand. The drawing, for example, of a bird on one side and a cage on the other would, when spun, produce the appearance of the bird in the cage. Another had a portrait of a bald-headed man on one side, a hairpiece on the other. Paris described the relation between retinal after-images and the operation of his device:

> An object was seen by the eye, in consequence of its image being
> delineated on the retina or optic nerve, which is situated on the

back part of the eye; and that it has been ascertained, by experiment, that the impression which the mind thus receives, lasts for
about the eighth part of a second after the image is removed . . . the
Thaumatrope depends upon the same optical principle; the
impression made on the retina by the image, which is delineated
on one side of the card, is not erased before that which is painted
on the opposite side is presented to the eye; and the consequence
is that you see both sides at once.[18]

Similar phenomena had been observed in earlier centuries merely by spin-
ning a coin and seeing both sides at the same time, but this was the first time
the phenomenon was given a scientific explanation *and* a device was produced to be sold as a popular entertainment. The simplicity of this "philosophical toy" made unequivocally clear both the fabricated and hallucinatory
nature of its image and the rupture between perception and its object.

Also in 1825, Peter Mark Roget, an English mathematician and the author
of the first thesaurus, published an account of his observations of railway train
wheels seen through the vertical bars of a fence. Roget pointed out the illusions that occurred under this circumstance—the spokes of the wheels
seemed to be either motionless or to be turning backward. "The deception
in the appearance of the spokes must arise from the circumstances of separate
parts only of each spoke being seen at the same moment . . . several portions
of one and the same line, seen through the intervals of the bars, form on the
retina the images of so many different radii."[19] Roget's observations suggested
to him how the location of an observer in relation to an intervening screen
could exploit the durational properties of retinal afterimages to create various
effects of motion. The physicist Michael Faraday explored similar phenomena,
particularly the experience of rapidly turning wheels that appeared to be moving slowly. In 1831, the year of his discovery of electromagnetic induction, he
produced his own device, later called the Faraday wheel, consisting of two

18.   See John A. Paris, *Philosophy in Sport Made Science in Earnest; Being an Attempt to
Illustrate the First Principles of Natural Philosophy by the Aid of Popular Toys and Sports*
(London, 1827), vol. 3, pp. 13–15.
19.   Peter Mark Roget, "Explanation of an optical deception in the appearance of the
spokes of a wheel seen through vertical apertures," *Philosophical Transactions of the Royal
Society,* 115 (1825), p. 135.

Use of phenakistiscope before a mirror.

spoked or slotted wheels mounted on the same axis. By varying the relation between the spokes of the two wheels relative to the eye of the viewer, the apparent motion of the further wheel could be modulated. Thus the experience of temporality itself is made susceptible to a range of external technical manipulations.

During the late 1820s the Belgian scientist Joseph Plateau also conducted a wide range of experiments with afterimages, some of which cost him his eyesight due to staring directly into the sun for extended periods. By 1828 he had worked with a Newton color wheel, demonstrating that the duration and quality of retinal afterimages varied with the intensity, color, time, and direction of the stimulus. He also made a calculation of the average time that such sensations lasted—about a third of a second. What is more, his research seemed to confirm the earlier speculations of Goethe and others that retinal afterimages do not simply dissipate uniformly, but go through a number of positive and negative states before vanishing. He made one of the most influential formulations of the theory of "persistence of vision."

> If several objects which differ sequentially in terms of form and
> position are presented one after the other to the eye in very brief

Phenakistiscopes. 1830s.

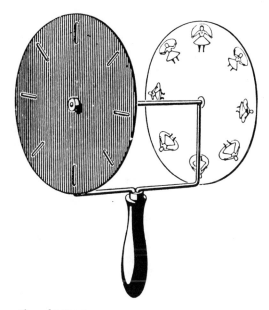

Phenakistiscope.

intervals and sufficiently close together, the impressions they produce on the retina will blend together without confusion and one
will believe that a single object is gradually changing form and
position.[20]

In the early 1830s Plateau constructed the phenakistiscope (literally, "decep-
tive view"), which incorporated his own research and that of Roget, Faraday,
and others. At its simplest it consisted of a single disc, divided into eight or
sixteen equal segments, each of which contained a small slitted opening and
a figure, representing one position in a sequence of movement. The side with
figures drawn on it was faced toward a mirror while the viewer stayed immobile as the disc turned. When an opening passed in front of the eye, it allowed
one to see the figure on the disc very briefly. The same effect occurs with each
of the slits. Because of retinal persistence, a series of images results that
appear to be in continuous motion before the eye. By 1833, commercial mod-

20.   Joseph Plateau, *Dissertation sur quelques propriétés des impressions,* thesis submitted at Liège, May 1829. Quoted in Georges Sadoul, *Histoire générale du cinéma.* Vol. 1:
L'invention du cinéma (Paris, 1948), p. 25.

els were being sold in London. By 1834 two similar devices appeared: the stroboscope, invented by the German mathematician Stampfer, and the zootrope or "wheel of life" of William G. Horner. The latter was a turning cylinder around which several spectators could view simultaneously a simulated action, often sequences of dancers, jugglers, boxers, or acrobats.

The details and background of these devices and inventors have been well documented elsewhere, but almost exclusively in the service of a history of cinema.[21] Film studies position them as the initial forms in an evolutionary technological development leading to the emergence of a single dominant form at the end of the century. Their fundamental characteristic is that they are not yet cinema, thus nascent, imperfectly designed forms. Obviously there is a connection between cinema and these machines of the 1830s, but it is often a dialectical relation of inversion and opposition, in which features of these earlier devices were negated or concealed. At the same time there is a tendency to conflate all optical devices in the nineteenth century as equally implicated in a vague collective drive to higher and higher standards of verisimilitude. Such an approach often ignores the conceptual and historical singularities of each device.

The empirical truth of the notion of "persistence of vision" as an explanation for the illusion of motion is irrelevant here.[22] What is important are the conditions and circumstances that allowed it to operate as an explanation and the historical subject/observer that it presupposed. The idea of persistence of

21.   See, for example, works as diverse as the following: C. W. Ceram, *Archaeology of the Cinema* (New York, 1965); Michael Chanan, *The Dream that Kicks: The Prehistory and Early Years of Cinema in Britain* (London, 1980), esp. pp. 54–65; Jean-Louis Comolli, "Technique et idéologie," *Cahiers du cinéma* no. 229 (May-June 1971), pp. 4–21; Jean Mitry, *Histoire du cinéma,* vol. 1 (Paris, 1967), pp. 21–27; Georges Sadoul, *Histoire générale du cinéma,* vol. 1, pp. 15–43; Steve Neale, *Cinema and Technology: Image, Sound, Colour* (Bloomington, 1985), pp. 9–32; and Leo Sauvage, *L'affaire Lumière: Enquête sur les origines du cinéma* (Paris, 1985), pp. 29–48. For another genealogical model, see Gilles Deleuze, *Cinema 1: The Movement-Image* (Minneapolis, 1986), pp. 4–5.
22.   Some recent studies have discussed the "myth" of persistence of vision. They tell us, not surprisingly, that recent neurophysiological research shows nineteenth-century explanations of fusion or blending of images to be an inadequate explanation for the perception of illusory motion. See Joseph and Barbara Anderson, "Motion Perception in Motion Pictures," and Bill Nichols and Susan J. Lederman, "Flicker and Motion in Film," both in *The Cinematic Apparatus,* ed. Teresa de Lauretis and Stephen Heath (London, 1980), pp. 76–95 and 96–105.

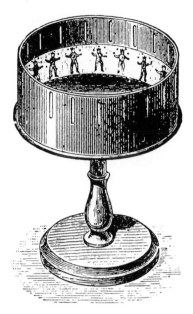

Zootrope. Mid-1830s.

vision is linked to two different sorts of studies. One is the kind of self-observation conducted first by Goethe, then by Purkinje, Plateau, Fechner, and others, in which the changing conditions of the observer's own retina was (or was
then believed to be) the object of investigation. The other source was the often
accidental observation of new forms of movement, in particular mechanized
wheels moving at high speeds. Purkinje and Roget both derived some of their
ideas from noting the appearance of train wheels in motion or regularly
spaced forms seen from a fast-moving train.[23] Faraday indicates that his experiments were suggested by a visit to a factory: "Being at the magnificent lead
mills of Messrs. Maltby, two cog-wheels were shown me moving with such
velocity that if the eye were . . . standing in such a position that one wheel

23.   See Nietzsche, *Human, All Too Human,* trans. R. J. Hollingdale (1878; Cambridge,
1986), p. 132: "With the tremendous acceleration of life, mind and eye have become accustomed to seeing and judging partially or inaccurately, and everyone is like the traveller who
gets to know a land and its people from a railway carriage." On the cultural impact and
"perceptual shock" of railroad travel, see Wolfgang Schivelbusch, *The Railway Journey:
Trains and Travel in the 19th Century,* trans. Anselm Hollo (New York, 1979), esp. pp. 145–
160.

appeared behind the other, there was immediately the distinct though shadowy resemblance of cogs moving slowly in one direction."[24] Like the study of afterimages, new experiences of speed and machine movement disclosed an increasing divergence between appearances and their external causes.

The phenakistiscope substantiates Walter Benjamin's claim that in the nineteenth century "technology has subjected the human sensorium to a complex kind of training." At the same time, it would be a mistake to accord new industrial techniques primacy in shaping or determining a new kind of observer.[25] While the phenakistiscope was of course a mode of popular entertainment, a leisure-time commodity purchasable by an expanding urban middle class, it also paralleled the format of the scientific devices used by Purkinje, Plateau, and others for the empirical study of subjective vision. That is, a form with which a new public consumed images of an illusory "reality" was isomorphic to the apparatuses used to accumulate knowledge about an observer. In fact, the very physical position required of the observer by the phenakistiscope bespeaks a confounding of three modes: an individual body that is at once a spectator, a subject of empirical research and observation, and an element of machine production. This is where Foucault's opposition between spectacle and surveillance becomes untenable; his two distinct models here collapse onto one another. The production of the observer in the nineteenth century coincided with new procedures of discipline and regulation. In each of the modes mentioned above, it is a question of a body aligned with and operating an assemblage of turning and regularly moving wheeled parts. The imperatives that generated a rational organization of time and movement in production simultaneously pervaded diverse spheres of social activity. A need for knowledge of the capacities of the eye and its regimentation dominated many of them.

Another phenomenon that corroborates this change in the position of the observer is the diorama, given its definitive form by Louis J. M. Daguerre in the early 1820s. Unlike the static panorama painting that first appeared in the 1790s, the diorama is based on the incorporation of an *immobile* observer

24   Quoted in Chanan, *The Dream that Kicks,* p. 61.
25.   Walter Benjamin, *Charles Baudelaire: A Lyric Poet in the Era of High Capitalism,*
trans. Harry Zohn (London, 1973), p. 126.

into a mechanical apparatus and a subjection to a predesigned temporal unfolding of optical experience.[26] The circular or semicircular panorama painting clearly broke with the localized point of view of perspective painting or the camera obscura, allowing the spectator an ambulatory ubiquity. One was compelled at the least to turn one's head (and eyes) to see the entire work. The multimedia diorama removed that autonomy from the observer, often situating the audience on a circular platform that was slowly moved, permitting views of different scenes and shifting light effects. Like the phenakistiscope or the zootrope, the diorama was a machine of wheels in motion, one in which the observer was a component. For Marx, one of the great technical innovations of the nineteenth century was the way in which the body was made adaptable to "the few main fundamental forms of motion."[27] But if the modernization of the observer involved the adaptation of the eye to rationalized forms of movement, such a change coincided with and was possible only because of an increasing abstraction of optical experience from a stable referent. Thus one feature of modernization in the nineteenth century was the "uprooting" of vision from the more inflexible representational system of the camera obscura.

Consider also the kaleidoscope, invented in 1815 by Sir David Brewster. With all the luminous possibilities suggested by Baudelaire and later Proust, the kaleidoscope seems radically unlike the rigid and disciplinary structure of the phenakistiscope, with its sequential repetition of regulated representations. For Baudelaire the kaleidoscope coincided with modernity itself; to become a "kaleidoscope gifted with consciousness" was the goal of "the lover of universal life." In his text it figured as a machine for the disintegration of a unitary subjectivity and for the scattering of desire into new shifting and

---

26.   An important study on the relation between the panorama and the diorama is Eric de Kuyper and Emile Poppe, "Voir et regarder," *Communications* 34 (1981), pp. 85–96. Other works include Stephan Oettermann, *Des Panorama* (Munich, 1980); Heinz Buddemeier, *Panorama, Diorama, Photographie: Entstehung und Wirkung neuer Medien im 19. Jahrhundert* (Munich, 1970); Helmut and Alison Gernsheim, *L. J. M. Daguerre: The History of the Diorama and the Daguerreotype* (New York, 1968); Dolf Sternberger, *Panorama of the 19th Century,* trans. Joachim Neugroschel (New York, 1977), pp. 7–16, 184–189; John Barnes, *Precursors of the Cinema: Peepshows, Panoramas and Dioramas* (St. Ives, 1967); and W. Neite, "The Cologne Diorama," *History of Photography* 3, no. 2 (April 1979), pp. 105–109.
27.   Karl Marx, *Capital,* vol. 1, p. 374.

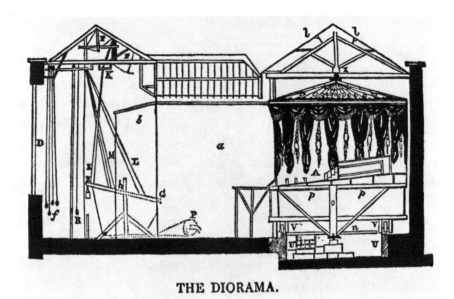

THE DIORAMA.

The London Diorama. 1823.

labile arrangements, by fragmenting any point of iconicity and disrupting stasis.

But for Marx and Engels, writing in the 1840s, the kaleidoscope had a very different function. The multiplicity that so seduced Baudelaire was for them a sham, a trick literally done with mirrors. Rather than producing something new the kaleidoscope simply repeated a single image. In their attack on Saint-Simon in *The German Ideology,* a "kaleidoscopic display" is "composed entirely of reflections of itself."[28] According to Marx and Engels, Saint-Simon pretends to be moving his reader from one idea to another, while actually holding to the same position throughout. We don't know how much Marx or Engels knew about the technical structure of the kaleidoscope but they allude to a crucial feature of it in their dissection of Saint-Simon's text. The kaleidoscope presents its viewer with a symmetrical repetition, and the breakup of Marx and Engels's page into two columns of quotations explicitly demonstrates Saint-Simon's maneuver of "self-reflection." The structural underpin-

28.   Karl Marx and Friedrich Engels, *The German Ideology,* ed. R. Pascal (New York, 1963), pp. 109–111.

Kaleidoscopes. Mid-nineteenth century.

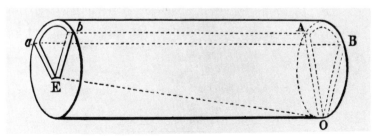

Position of mirrors inside kaleidoscope.

nings of the kaleidoscope are bipolar and paradoxically the characteristic effect of shimmering dissolution is produced by a simple binary reflective setup (it consists of two plane mirrors extending the length of the tube, inclined at an angle of sixty degrees, or any angle that is a sub-multiple of four right angles). The rotation of this invariant symmetrical format is what generates the appearance of decomposition and proliferation.

For Sir David Brewster, the justification for making the kaleidoscope was productivity and efficiency. He saw it as a mechanical means for the reformation of art according to an industrial paradigm. Since symmetry was the basis of beauty in nature and visual art, he declared, the kaleidoscope was aptly suited to produce art through "the inversion and multiplication of simple forms."

> If we reflect further on the nature of the designs thus composed, and on the methods which must be employed in their composition, the Kaleidoscope will assume the character of the highest class of machinery, which improves at the same time that it abridges the exertions of individuals. There are few machines, indeed, which rise higher above the operations of human skill. It will create in an hour, what a thousand artists could not invent in the course of a year; and while it works with such unexampled rapidity, it works also with a corresponding beauty and precision.[29]

Brewster's proposal of infinite serial production seems far removed from Baudelaire's image of the dandy as "a kaleidoscope gifted with consciousness." But the abstraction necessary for Brewster's industrial delirium is made possible by the same forces of modernization that allowed Baudelaire to use the kaleidoscope as a model for the kinetic experience of "the multiplicity of life itself and the flickering grace of all its elements."[30]

The most significant form of visual imagery in the nineteenth century, with the exception of photographs, was the stereoscope.[31] It is easily forgotten

29.   Sir David Brewster, *The Kaleidoscope: Its History, Theory, and Construction* (1819; rpt. London, 1858), pp. 134–136.
30.   Charles Baudelaire, "Le peintre de la vie moderne," in *Oeuvres Complètes* (Paris, 1961), p. 1161. In the same volume see Baudelaire's discussion of the stereoscope and the phenakistiscope in his 1853 essay "Morale du joujou," pp. 524–530.
31.   There are few serious cultural or historical studies of the stereoscope. Some helpful

Second Empire interior with lenses, magic lantern, and stereoscope.

now how pervasive was the experience of the stereoscope and how for decades it defined a major mode of experiencing photographically produced images. This too is a form whose history has thus far been confounded with that of another phenomenon, in this case photography. Yet as I indicated in my introduction, its conceptual structure and the historical circumstances of its invention are thoroughly independent of photography. Although distinct from the optical devices that represented the illusion of movement, the stereoscope is nonetheless part of the same reorganization of the observer, the same relations of knowledge and power, that those devices implied.

Of primary concern here is the period during which the technical and theoretical principles of the stereoscope were developed, rather than the issue of its effects once it was distributed throughout a sociocultural field. Only after 1850 did its wide commercial diffusion throughout North America and Europe occur.[32] The origins of the stereoscope are intertwined with research in the 1820s and 1830s on subjective vision and more generally within the field of nineteenth-century physiology already discussed. The two figures most closely associated with its invention, Charles Wheatstone and Sir David Brewster, had already written extensively on optical illusions, color theory, afterimages and other visual phenomena. Wheatstone was in fact the translator of Purkinje's major 1823 dissertation on afterimages and subjective vision, published in English in 1830. A few years later Brewster summarized available research on optical devices and subjective vision.

The stereoscope is also inseparable from early nineteenth-century debates about the perception of space, which were to continue unresolved indefinitely. Was space an innate form or was it something recognized through the learning of cues after birth? The Molyneux problem had been transposed to a different century for very different solutions. But the question that troubled the nineteenth century had never really been a central problem before.

---

works are: Edward W. Earle, ed., *Points of View: The Stereograph in America: A Cultural History* (Rochester, 1979); A. T. Gill, "Early Stereoscopes," *The Photographic Journal* 109 (1969), pp. 545–599, 606–614, 641–651; and Rosalind Krauss, "Photography's Discursive Spaces: Landscape/View," *Art Journal* 42 (Winter 1982), pp. 311–319.

32.   By 1856, two years after its founding, the London Stereoscopic Company alone had sold over half a million viewers. See Helmut and Alison Gernsheim, *The History of Photography* (London, 1969), p. 191.

Binocular disparity, the self-evident fact that each eye sees a slightly different image, had been a familiar phenomenon since antiquity. Only in the 1830s does it become crucial for scientists to define the seeing body as essentially binocular, to quantify precisely the angular differential of the optical axis of each eye, and to specify the physiological basis for disparity. The question that preoccupied researchers was this: given that an observer perceives with each eye a different image, *how* are they experienced as single or unitary? Before 1800, even when the question was asked it was more as a curiosity, never a central problem. Two alternative explanations had been offered for centuries: one proposed that we never saw anything except with one eye at a time; the other was a projection theory articulated by Kepler, and proposed as late as the 1750s, which asserted that each eye projects an object to its actual location.[33] But in the nineteenth century the unity of the visual field could not be so easily predicated.

By the late 1820s physiologists were seeking anatomical evidence in the structure of the optical chiasma, the point behind the eyes where the nerve fibers leading from the retina to the brain cross each other, carrying half of the nerves from each retina to each side of the brain.[34] But such physiological evidence was relatively inconclusive at that time. Wheatstone's conclusions in 1833 came out of the successful measurement of binocular parallax, or the degree to which the angle of the axis of each eye differed when focused on the same point. The human organism, he claimed, had the capacity under most conditions to synthesize retinal disparity into a single unitary image. While this seems obvious from our own standpoint, Wheatstone's work marked a major break from older explanations (or often disregard) of the binocular body.

The form of the stereoscope is linked to some of Wheatstone's initial findings: his research concerned the visual experience of objects relatively close to the eye.

> When an object is viewed at so great a distance that the optic axes of both eyes are sensibly parallel when directed towards it, the per-

33.   See, for example, William Porterfield, *A Treatise on the Eye, the Manner and Phenomena of Vision* (Edinburgh, 1759), p. 285.
34.   See R. L. Gregory, *Eye and Brain: The Psychology of Seeing,* 3rd ed. (New York, 1979), p. 45.

spective projections of it, seen by each eye separately, and the appearance to the two eyes is precisely the same as when the object is seen by one eye only.[35]

Instead Wheatstone was preoccupied with objects close enough to the observer so that the optic axes had *different* angles.

> When the object is placed so near the eyes that to view it the optic axes must converge . . . a different perspective projection of it is seen by each eye, and these perspectives are more dissimilar as the convergence of the optic axes becomes greater.[36]

Thus physical proximity brings binocular vision into play as an operation of reconciling disparity, of making two distinct views appear as one. This is what links the stereoscope with other devices in the 1830s like the phenakistiscope. Its "realism" presupposes perceptual experience to be essentially an apprehension of differences. The relation of the observer to the object is not one of identity but an experience of disjunct or divergent images. Helmholtz's influential epistemology was based on such a "differential hypothesis."[37] Both Wheatstone and Brewster indicated that the fusion of pictures viewed in a stereoscope took place over time and that their convergence might not actually be secure. According to Brewster,

> the relief is not obtained from the mere combination or super-position of the two dissimilar pictures. The superposition is effected by turning each eye upon the object, but the relief is given by the play of the optic axes in uniting, in rapid *succession,* similar points of the two pictures. . . . Though the pictures apparently coalesce, yet the relief is given by the subsequent play of the optic

35.   Charles Wheatstone, "Contributions to the physiology of vision—Part the first. On some remarkable, and hitherto unobserved, phenomena of binocular vision," in *Brewster and Wheatstone on Vision,* ed. Nicholas J. Wade (London, 1983), p. 65.
36.   Wheatstone, "Contributions to a physiology of vision," p. 65.
37.   Hermann von Helmholtz, "The Facts in Perception," *Epistemological Writings,* ed. Moritz Schlick (Boston, 1977), p. 133: "Our acquaintance with the visual field can be acquired by observation of the images during the movements of our eyes, provided only that there exists, between otherwise qualitatively alike retinal sensations, some or other perceptible difference corresponding to the difference between distinct places on the retina."

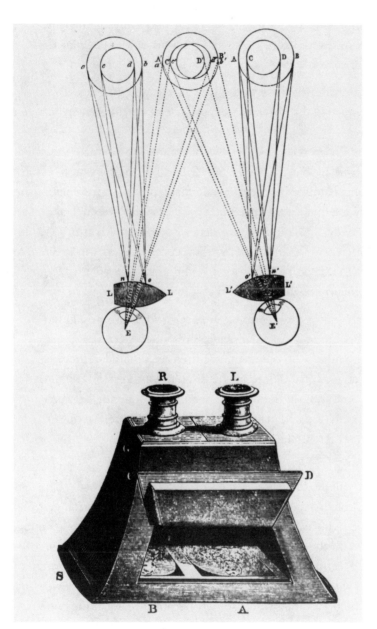

David Brewster's lenticular stereoscope. 1849.

axes varying themselves *successively* upon, and unifying, the similar points in each picture that correspond to different distances
from the observer.[38]

Brewster thus confirms there never really is a stereoscopic image, that it is a
conjuration, an effect of the observer's experience of the differential between
two other images.

In devising the stereoscope, Wheatstone aimed to simulate the actual
presence of a physical object or scene, not to discover another way to exhibit
a print or drawing. Painting had been an adequate form of representation, he
asserts, but only for images of objects at a great distance. When a landscape
is presented to a viewer, "if those circumstances which would disturb the illusion are excluded," we could mistake the representation for reality. He
declares that up to this point in history it is impossible for an artist to give a
faithful representation of any *near* solid object.

> When the painting and the object are seen with both eyes, in the
> case of the painting two similar objects are projected on the retina,
> in the case of the solid object the pictures are dissimilar; there is
> therefore an essential difference between the impressions on the
> organs of sensation in the two cases, and consequently between
> the perceptions formed in the mind; the painting therefore cannot
> be confounded with the solid object.[39]

What he seeks, then, is a complete equivalence of stereoscopic image and
object. Not only will the invention of the stereoscope overcome the deficiencies of painting but also those of the diorama, which Wheatstone singles out.
The diorama, he believed, was too bound up in the techniques of painting,
which depended for their illusory effects on the depiction of distant subjects.
The stereoscope, on the contrary, provided a form in which "vividness" of
effect increased with the apparent proximity of the object to the viewer, and
the impression of three-dimensional solidity became greater as the optic axes
of each diverged. Thus the desired effect of the stereoscope was not simply

38.   Sir David Brewster, *The Stereoscope: Its History, Theory, and Construction* (London,
1856), p. 53 (emphasis in original).
39.   Charles Wheatstone, "Contributions to the Physiology of Vision," in *Brewster and
Wheatstone on Vision,* p. 66.

Stereoscopes in use. Second Empire.

likeness, but immediate, apparent *tangibility*. But it is a tangibility that has been transformed into a purely visual experience, of a kind that Diderot could never have imagined. The "reciprocal assistance" between sight and touch Diderot specified in *Letters on the Blind* is no longer operative. Even as sophisticated a student of vision as Helmholtz could write, in the 1850s,

> these stereoscopic photographs are so true to nature and so lifelike
> in their portrayal of material things, that after viewing such a pic-
> ture and recognizing in it some object like a house, for instance,
> we get the impression, when we actually do see the object, that we
> have already seen it before and are more or less familiar with it. In
> cases of this kind, the actual view of the thing itself does not add
> anything new or more accurate to the previous apperception we
> got from the picture, so far at least as mere form relations are
> concerned.[40]

No other form of representation in the nineteenth century had so conflated the real with the optical. We will never really know what the stereoscope looked like to a nineteenth-century viewer or recover a stance from which it could seem an equivalent for a "natural vision." There is even something "uncanny" in Helmholtz's conviction that a picture of a house could be so real that we feel "we have already seen it before." Since it is obviously impossible to reproduce stereoscopic effects here on a printed page, it is necessary to analyze closely the nature of this illusion for which such claims were made, to look through the lenses of the device itself.

First it must be emphasized that the "reality effect" of the stereoscope was highly variable. Some stereoscopic images produce little or no three-dimensional effect: for instance, a view across an empty plaza of a building facade, or a view of a distant landscape with few intervening elements. Also, images that elsewhere are standard demonstrations of perspectival recession, such as a road or a railroad track extending to a centrally located vanishing point, produce little impression of depth. Pronounced stereoscopic effects depend on the presence of objects or obtrusive forms in the near or middle ground; that is, there must be enough points in the image that require sig-

40.   Helmholtz, *Physiological Optics,* vol. 3, p. 303.

nificant changes in the angle of convergence of the optical axes. Thus the most intense experience of the stereoscopic image coincides with an object-filled space, with a material plenitude that bespeaks a nineteenth-century bourgeois horror of the void; and there are endless quantities of stereo cards showing interiors crammed with bric-a-brac, densely filled museum sculpture galleries, and congested city views.

But in such images the depth is essentially different from anything in painting or photography. We are given an insistent sense of "in front of" and "in back of" that seems to organize the image as a sequence of receding planes. And in fact the fundamental organization of the stereoscopic image is *planar.*[41] We perceive individual elements as flat, cutout forms arrayed either nearer or further from us. But the experience of space between these objects (planes) is not one of gradual and predictable recession; rather, there is a vertiginous uncertainty about the distance separating forms. Compared to the strange insubstantiality of objects and figures located in the middle ground, the absolutely airless space surrounding them has a disturbing palpability. There are some superficial similarities between the stereoscope and classical stage design, which synthesizes flats and real extensive space into an illusory scene. But theatrical space is still perspectival in that the movement of actors on a stage generally rationalizes the relation between points.

In the stereoscopic image there is a derangement of the conventional functioning of optical cues. Certain planes or surfaces, even though composed of indications of light or shade that normally designate volume, are perceived as flat; other planes that normally would be read as two-dimensional, such as a fence in a foreground, seem to occupy space aggressively. Thus stereoscopic relief or depth has no unifying logic or order. If perspective implied a homogeneous and potentially metric space, the stereoscope discloses a fundamentally disunified and aggregate field of disjunct elements. Our eyes never traverse the image in a full apprehension of the three-dimensionality of the entire field, but in terms of a localized experience of separate areas. When we look head-on at a photograph or painting our eyes remain at a single angle of convergence, thus endowing the image surface with an optical unity. The reading or scanning of a stereo image, however, is an accumulation of dif-

41.   See Krauss, "Photography's Discursive Spaces," p. 313.

ferences in the degree of optical convergence, thereby producing a perceptual effect of a patchwork of different intensities of relief within a single image.
Our eyes follow a choppy and erratic path into its depth: it is an assemblage
of local zones of three-dimensionality, zones imbued with a hallucinatory clarity, but which when taken together never coalesce into a homogeneous field.
It is a world that simply does not communicate with that which produced
baroque scenography or the city views of Canaletto and Bellotto. Part of the
fascination of these images is due to this immanent disorder, to the fissures
that disrupt its coherence. The stereoscope could be said to constitute what
Gilles Deleuze calls a "Riemann space," after the German mathematician
Georg Riemann (1826–1866). "Each vicinity in a Riemann space is like a shred
of Euclidian space but the linkage between one vicinity and the next is not
defined. . . . Riemann space at its most general thus presents itself as an amor-
phous collection of pieces that are juxtaposed but not attached to each other."[42]

A range of nineteenth-century painting also manifests some of these features of stereoscopic imagery. Courbet's *Ladies of the Village* (1851), with its
much-noted discontinuity of groups and planes, suggests the aggregate space
of the stereoscope, as do similar elements of *The Meeting (Bonjour, M. Courbet)* (1854). Works by Manet, such as *The Execution of Maximillian* (1867) and
View of the International Exhibition (1867), and certainly Seurat's *Sunday
Afternoon on the Island of La Grande Jatte* (1884–86) also are built up piece-
meal out of local and disjunct areas of spatial coherence, of both modeled
depth and cutout flatness. Numerous other examples could be mentioned,
perhaps going back as early as the landscapes of Wilhelm von Köbell, with
their unsettling hyperclarity and abrupt adjacency of foreground and distant
background. I am certainly not proposing a causal relation of *any* sort
between these two forms, and I would be dismayed if I prompted anyone to
determine if Courbet owned a stereoscope. Instead I am suggesting that *both*
the "realism" of the stereoscope and the "experiments" of certain painters
were equally bound up in a much broader transformation of the observer that
allowed the emergence of this new optically constructed space. The stereoscope and Cézanne have far more in common than one might assume. Paint-

42.   Gilles Deleuze and Félix Guattari, *A Thousand Plateaus*, p. 485.

ing, and early modernism in particular, had no special claims in the renovation of vision in the nineteenth century.

The stereoscope as a means of representation was inherently *obscene,* in the most literal sense. It shattered the *scenic* relationship between viewer and object that was intrinsic to the fundamentally theatrical setup of the camera obscura. The very functioning of the stereoscope depended, as indicated above, on the visual priority of the object closest to the viewer and on the absence of any mediation between eye and image.[43] It was a fulfillment of what Walter Benjamin saw as central in the visual culture of modernity: "Day by day the need becomes greater to take possession of the object—from the closest proximity—in an image and the reproduction of an image."[44] It is no coincidence that the stereoscope became increasingly synonymous with erotic and pornographic imagery in the course of the nineteenth century. The very effects of tangibility that Wheatstone had sought from the beginning were quickly turned into a mass form of ocular possession. Some have speculated that the very close association of the stereoscope with pornography was in part responsible for its social demise as a mode of visual consumption. Around the turn of the century sales of the device supposedly dwindled because it became linked with "indecent" subject matter. Although the reasons for the collapse of the stereoscope lie elsewhere, as I will suggest shortly, the simulation of tangible three-dimensionality hovers uneasily at the limits of acceptable verisimilitude.[45]

If photography preserved an ambivalent (and superficial) relation to the codes of monocular space and geometrical perspective, the relation of the stereoscope to these older forms was one of annihilation, not compromise. Charles Wheatstone's question in 1838 was: "What would be the visual effect of simultaneously presenting to each eye, instead of the object itself, its pro-

43.   See Florence de Mèredieu, "De l'obscénité photographique," *Traverses* 29 (October 1983), pp. 86–94.
44.   Walter Benjamin, "A Small History of Photography," in *One Way Street,* trans. Edmund Jephcott and Kingsley Shorter (London, 1979), pp. 240–257.
45.   The ambivalence with which twentieth-century audiences have received 3-D movies and holography suggests the enduring problematic nature of such techniques. Christian Metz discusses the idea of an optimal point on either side of which the impression of reality tends to decrease, in his *Film Language* (New York, 1974), pp. 3–15.

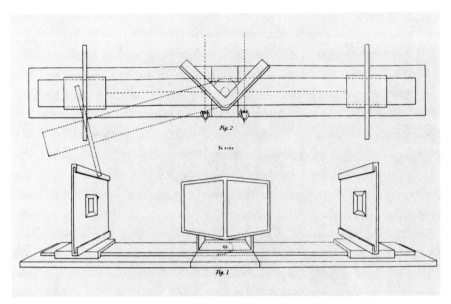

Diagram of the operation of the Wheatstone stereoscope.

jection on a plane surface as it appears to that eye?" The stereoscopic spectator sees neither the identity of a copy nor the coherence guaranteed by the frame of a window. Rather, what appears is the technical reconstitution of an already reproduced world fragmented into *two* nonidentical models, models that precede any experience of their subsequent perception as unified or tangible. It is a radical repositioning of the observer's relation to visual representation. The institutionalization of this decentered observer and the stereoscope's dispersed and multiplied sign severed from a point of external reference indicate a greater break with a classical observer than that which occurs later in the century in the realm of painting. The stereoscope signals an eradication of "the point of view" around which, for several centuries, meanings had been assigned reciprocally to an observer and the object of his or her vision. There is no longer the possibility of perspective under such a technique of beholding. The relation of observer to image is no longer to an object quantified in relation to a position in space, but rather to two dissimilar images whose position simulates the anatomical structure of the observer's body.

To fully appreciate the rupture signified by the stereoscope it is important to consider the original device, the so-called Wheatstone stereoscope. In order to view images with this device, an observer placed his eyes directly in front of two plane mirrors set ninety degrees to one another. The images to be viewed were held in slots on either side of the observer, and thus were spatially completely separated from each other. Unlike the Brewster stereo-scope, invented in the late 1840s, or the familiar Holmes viewer, invented in 1861, the Wheatstone model made clear the atopic nature of the perceived stereoscopic image, the disjunction between experience and its cause. The later models allowed the viewer to believe that he or she was looking forward *at* something "out there." But the Wheatstone model left the hallucinatory and fabricated nature of the experience undisguised. It did not support what Roland Barthes called "the referential illusion."[46] There simply was nothing "out there." The illusion of relief or depth was thus a subjective event and the observer coupled with the apparatus was the agent of synthesis or fusion.

Like the phenakistiscope and other nonprojective optical devices, the stereoscope also required the corporeal adjacency and immobility of the observer. They are part of a nineteenth-century modulation in the relation between eye and optical apparatus. During the seventeenth and eighteenth centuries that relationship had been essentially metaphoric: the eye and the camera obscura or the eye and the telescope or microscope were allied by a conceptual similarity, in which the authority of an ideal eye remained unchal-lenged.[47] Beginning in the nineteenth century, the relation between eye and optical apparatus becomes one of metonymy: both were now contiguous instruments on the same plane of operation, with varying capabilities and fea-tures.[48] The limits and deficiencies of one will be complemented by the capac-ities of the other and vice versa. The optical apparatus undergoes a shift comparable to that of the tool as described by Marx: "From the moment that the tool proper is taken from man, and fitted into a mechanism, a machine

46. See Roland Barthes, "The Reality Effect," in *The Rustle of Language,* trans. Richard Howard (New York, 1986), pp. 141–148.

47. On the telescope as metaphor in Galileo, Kepler, and others see Timothy J. Riess, *The Discourse of Modernism* (Ithaca, 1980), pp. 25–29.

48. "In Metonymy, phenomena are implicitly apprehended as bearing relationships to one another in the modality of part-part relationships, on the basis of which one can effect a *reduction* of one of the parts to the status of an aspect or function of the other." Hayden White, *Metahistory: The Historical Imagination in Nineteenth Century Europe* (Baltimore, 1973), p. 35.

Manufacture of stereographs. Paris, late 1850s.

takes the place of a mere implement."[49] In this sense, other optical instruments of the seventeenth and eighteenth centuries, like peep shows, Claude glasses, and print viewing boxes had the status of tools. In the older handicraft-based work, Marx explained, a workman "makes use of a tool," that is, the tool had a metaphoric relation to the innate powers of the human subject.[50] In the factory, Marx contended, the machine makes use of man by subjecting him to a relation of contiguity, of part to other parts, and of exchangeability. He is quite specific about the new metonymic status of the human subject: "As soon as man, instead of working with an implement on the subject of his labour, becomes merely the motive power of an implement-machine, it is a mere accident that motive power takes the disguise of human muscle; and it may equally well take the form of wind, water, or steam."[51] Georges Canguilhem makes an important distinction between eighteenth-century utilitarianism, which derived its idea of utility from its definition of man as toolmaker, and the instrumentalism of the human sciences in the nineteenth century, which is based on "one implicit postulate: that the nature of man is to be a tool, that his vocation is to be set in his place and to be set to work."[52] Although "set to work" may sound inappropriate in a discussion of optical devices, the apparently passive observer of the stereoscope and phenakistiscope, by virtue of specific

49.   Karl Marx, *Capital*, vol. 1, trans. Samuel Moore and Edward Aveling (New York, 1967), p. 374.
50.   Marx, *Capital*, vol. 1, p. 422. J. D. Bernal has noted that the instrumental capacities of the telescope and microscope remained remarkably undeveloped during the seventeenth and eighteenth centuries. Until the nineteenth century, the microscope "remained more amusing and instructive, in the philosophical sense, than of scientific and practical value." *Science in History, Vol. 2: The Scientific and Industrial Revolutions* (Cambridge, Mass., 1971), pp. 464–469.
51.   Marx, *Capital*, vol. 1, p. 375.
52.   Georges Canguilhem, "Qu'est-ce que la psychologie," *Etudes d'histoire et de philosophie des sciences* (Paris, 1983), p. 378. See also Gilles Deleuze and Félix Guattari, *A Thousand Plateaus*, p. 490: "During the nineteenth century a two-fold elaboration was undertaken: of a physioscientific concept of Work (weight-height, force-displacement), and of a socioeconomic concept of labor-power or abstract labor (a homogenous abstract quantity applicable to all work and susceptible to multiplication and division). There was a profound link between physics and sociology: society furnished an economic standard of measure for work, and physics as 'mechanical currency' for it. . . . Impose the Work Model upon every activity, translate every act into possible or virtual work, discipline free action, or else (which amounts to the same thing) relegate it to 'leisure,' which exists only by reference to work."

physiological capacities, was in fact made into a producer of forms of verisimilitude. And what the observer produced, again and again, was the effortless transformation of the dreary parallel images of flat stereo cards into a tantalizing apparition of depth. The content of the images is far less important than the inexhaustible routine of moving from one card to the next and producing the same effect, repeatedly, mechanically. And each time, the mass-produced and monotonous cards are transubstantiated into a compulsory and seductive vision of the "real."

A crucial feature of these optical devices of the 1830s and 1840s is the undisguised nature of their operational structure and the form of subjection they entail. Even though they provide access to "the real," they make no claim that the real is anything other than a mechanical production. The optical experiences they manufacture are clearly disjunct from the images used in the device. They refer as much to the functional interaction of body and machine as they do to external objects, no matter how "vivid" the quality of the illusion. So when the phenakistiscope and the stereoscope eventually disappeared, it was not as part of a smooth process of invention and improvement, but rather because these earlier forms were no longer adequate to current needs and uses.

One reason for their obsolescence was that they were insufficiently "phantasmagoric," a word that Adorno, Benjamin, and others have used to describe forms of representation after 1850. Phantasmagoria was a name for a specific type of magic-lantern performance in the 1790s and early 1800s, one that used back projection to keep an audience unaware of the lanterns. Adorno takes the word to indicate

> the occultation of production by means of the outward appearance
> of the product . . . this outer appearance can lay claim to the status
> of being. Its perfection is at the same time the perfection of the illu-
> sion that the work of art is a reality *sui generis* that constitutes itself
> in the realm of the absolute without having to renounce its claim
> to image the world.[53]

53.   Theodor Adorno, *In Search of Wagner,* trans. Rodney Livingstone (London, 1981), p. 85. On Adorno and the phantasmagoria, see Andreas Huyssen, *After the Great Divide: Modernism, Mass Culture, Postmodernism* (Bloomington, 1986), pp. 34–42. See also Rolf

But the effacement or mystification of a machine's operation was precisely what David Brewster hoped to overcome with his kaleidoscope and stereoscope. He optimistically saw the spread of scientific ideas in the nineteenth century undermining the possibility of phantasmagoric effects, and he overlapped the history of civilization with the development of tehnologies of illusion and apparition.[54] For Brewster, a Scottish Calvinist, the maintenance of barbarism, tyranny, and popery had always been founded on closely guarded knowledge of optics and acoustics, the secrets by which priestly and higher castes ruled. But his implied program, the democratization and mass dissemination of techniques of illusion, simply collapsed that older model of power onto a single human subject, transforming each observer into simultaneously the magician and the deceived.

Even in the later Holmes stereoscope, the "concealment of the process of production" did not fully occur.[55] Clearly the stereoscope was dependent on a physical engagement with the apparatus that became increasingly unacceptable, and the composite, synthetic nature of the stereoscopic image could never be fully effaced. An apparatus openly based on a principle of disparity, on a "binocular" body, and on an illusion patently derived from the binary referent of the stereoscopic card of paired images, gave way to a form that preserved the referential illusion more fully than anything before it. Photography defeated the stereoscope as a mode of visual consumption as well because it recreated and perpetuated the fiction that the "free" subject of the camera obscura was still viable. Photographs seemed to be a continuation of older "naturalistic" pictorial codes, but only because their dominant conventions were restricted to a narrow range of technical possibilities (that is, shutter speeds and lens openings that rendered elapsed time invisible and recorded

---

Tiedemann, "Dialectics at a Standstill: Approaches to the Passagen-Werk," in *On Walter Benjamin: Critical Essays and Recollections,* ed. Gary Smith (Cambridge, Mass., 1988), pp. 276–279. For the technical and cultural history of the original phantasmagoria, see Terry Castle, "Phantasmagoria: Spectral Technology and the Metaphorics of Modern Reverie," *Critical Inquiry* 15 (Autumn 1988), pp. 26–61; Erik Barnouw, *The Magician and the Cinema* (Oxford, 1981); and Martin Quigley, Jr., *Magic Shadows: The Story of the Origin of Motion Pictures,* pp. 75–79.

54.   Sir David Brewster, *Letters on Natural Magic* (New York, 1832), pp. 15–21.

55.   This device is described by its inventor in Oliver Wendell Holmes, "The Stereoscope and the Stereograph," *Atlantic Monthly* 3, no. 20 (June 1859), pp. 738–748.

Holmes stereoscope. 1870s.

Column stereoscope. 1870s.

Phantasmagoria. Mid-nineteenth century.

objects in focus).[56] But photography had already abolished the inseparability of observer and camera obscura, bound together by a single point of view, and made the new camera an apparatus fundamentally independent of the spectator, yet which masqueraded as a transparent and incorporeal intermediary between observer and world. The prehistory of the spectacle *and* the "pure perception" of modernism are lodged in the newly discovered territory of a fully embodied viewer, but the eventual triumph of both depends on the denial of the body, its pulsings and phantasms, as the ground of vision.[57]

56.   For the disruptive effect of Muybridge and Marey on nineteenth-century codes of "naturalistic" representation, see Noël Burch, "Charles Baudelaire versus Doctor Frankenstein," *Afterimage* 8–9 (Spring 1981), pp. 4–21.

57.   On the problem of modernism, vision, and the body, see the recent work of Rosalind Krauss: "Antivision," *October* 36 (Spring 1986), pp. 147–154; "The Blink of an Eye," in *The States of Theory: History, Art, and Critical Discourse,* ed. David Caroll (New York, 1990), pp. 175–199; and "The Impulse to See," in *Vision and Visuality,* ed. Hal Foster (Seattle, 1988), pp. 51–75.

... the nineteenth century, still the most obscure of all the centuries of the modern age up to now.

—Martin Heidegger

Allergic to any relapse into magic, art is part and parcel of the disenchant-ment of the world, to use Max Weber's term. It is inextricably intertwined with rationalization. What means and productive methods art has at its disposal are all derived from this nexus.

—Theodor Adorno

The collapse of the camera obscura as a model for the condition of an observer was part of a process of modernization, even as the camera itself had been an element of an earlier modernity, helping define a "free," private, and individualized subject in the seventeenth century. By the early 1800s, how-ever, the rigidity of the camera obscura, its linear optical system, its fixed posi-tions, its identification of perception and object, were all too inflexible and immobile for a rapidly changing set of cultural and political requirements. Obviously artists in the seventeenth and eighteenth centuries had made countless attempts to operate outside the constraints of the camera obscura and other techniques for the rationalization of vision, but always within a highly delimited terrain of experimentation. It is only in the early nineteenth century that the juridical model of the camera loses its preeminent authority. Vision is no longer subordinated to an exterior image of the true or the right. The eye is no longer what predicates a "real world."

The work of Goethe, Schopenhauer, Ruskin, and Turner and many others are all indications that by 1840 the process of perception itself had become, in various ways, a primary object of vision. For it was this very process that the functioning of the camera obscura kept invisible. Nowhere else is the breakdown of the perceptual model of the camera obscura more decisively evident than in the late work of Turner. Seemingly out of nowhere, his painting of the late 1830s and 1840s signals the irrevocable loss of a fixed source of light, the dissolution of a cone of light rays, and the collapse of the distance separating an observer from the site of optical experience. Instead of the immediate and unitary apprehension of an image, our experience of a Turner painting is lodged amidst an inescapable temporality. Hence Lawrence Gowing's account of Turner's concern with "the indefinite transmission and dispersal of light by an infinite series of reflections from an endless variety of surfaces and materials, each contributing its own colour that mingles with every other, penetrating ultimately to every recess, reflected everywhere."[1] The sfumato of Leonardo, which had generated during the previous three centuries a counter-practice to the dominance of geometrical optics, is suddenly and overwhelmingly triumphant in Turner. But the substantiality he gives to the void between objects and his challenge to the integrity and identity of forms now coincides with a new physics: the science of fields and thermodynamics.[2]

The new status of the observer signaled by Turner is perhaps best discussed in terms of his celebrated relationship to the sun.[3] Just as the sun

1.   Lawrence Gowing, *Turner: Imagination and Reality* (New York, 1966), p. 21.
2.   Turner's break with Newtonian and Euclidian models of space and form is discussed in Karl Kroeber, "Romantic Historicism: The Temporal Sublime," in *Images of Romanticism: Verbal and Visual Affinities,* ed. Karl Kroeber and William Walling (New Haven, 1978), pp. 163–165, and in Michel Serres, "Turner traduit Carnot," in *La traduction* (Paris, 1974), pp. 233–242.
3.   Turner's relation to the sun is discussed in Ronald Paulson, "Turner's Graffiti: The Sun and Its Glosses," in *Images of Romanticism*, pp. 167–188; Jack Lindsay, *Turner: His Life*

described by classical mechanics was displaced by new notions of heat, time, death, and entropy, so the sun presupposed by the camera obscura (that is, a sun that could only be indirectly re-presented to a human eye) was transformed by the position of a new artist-observer.[4] In Turner all of the mediations that previously had distanced and protected an observer from the dangerous brilliance of the sun are cast off. The exemplary figures of Kepler and Newton employed the camera obscura precisely to avoid looking directly into the sun while seeking to gain knowledge of it or of the light it propagated. In Descartes's *La dioptrique,* as discussed earlier, the form of the camera was a defense against the madness and unreason of dazzlement.[5]

Turner's direct confrontation with the sun, however, dissolves the very possibility of representation that the camera obscura was meant to ensure. His solar preoccupations were "visionary" in that he made central in his work the retinal processes of vision; and it was the carnal embodiment of sight that the camera obscura denied or repressed. In one of Turner's great later paintings, the 1843 *Light and Colour (Goethe's Theory)—The Morning After the Deluge,* the collapse of the older model of representation is complete: the view of the sun that had dominated so many of Turner's previous images now becomes a fusion of eye and sun.[6] On one hand it stands as an impossible image of a luminescence that can only be blinding and that has never been seen, but it also resembles an afterimage of that engulfing illumination. If the circular structure of this painting and others of the same period mimic the shape of the sun, they also correspond with the pupil of the eye and the retinal field

---

and Work (New York, 1966), pp. 210–213; and Martin D. Paley, *The Apocalyptic Sublime* (New Haven, 1985), pp. 143–170.

4.   On the cultural effects of these new concepts, see Krzysztof Pomian, *L'ordre du temps* (Paris, 1984), pp. 300–305.

5.   See Michel Foucault, *Madness and Civilization: A History of Insanity in the Age of Reason,* trans. Richard Howard (New York, 1973), p. 108: "Dazzlement is night in broad daylight, the darkness that rules at the very heart of what is excessive in light's radiance. Dazzled reason opens its eyes upon the sun, and sees *nothing,* that is, it does not see . . ."

6.   The extent to which Turner was influenced by Goethe's writings on physiological optics is uncertain. That Turner was clearly aware of the physiological power of complementary colors is asserted in Gerald E. Finley, "Turner: An Early Experiment with Colour Theory," *Journal of the Warburg and Courtauld Institute* 30 (1967), pp. 357–366. See also John Gage, "Turner's Annotated Books: Goethe's 'Theory of Colours,'" *Turner Studies* 4 (Winter 1982), pp. 34–52.

J. M. W. Turner. Light and Colour (Goethe's Theory)—The Morning After the Deluge. *1843.*

on which the temporal experience of an afterimage unfolds. Through the afterimage the sun is made to belong to the body, and the body in fact takes over as the source of its effects. It is perhaps in this sense that Turner's suns may be said to be self-portraits.[7]

But Turner was not alone in the nineteenth century with his visionary relation to the sun. Three scientific figures already mentioned in this study, Sir David Brewster, Joseph Plateau, and Gustav Fechner, all severely damaged their eyesight by staring into the sun in the course of research on retinal afterimages.[8] Plateau, inventor of the phenakistiscope, went blind permanently. Though as scientists their immediate aims obviously differed from those of Turner, on a more important level theirs too was a shared discovery of the "visionary" capacities of the body, and we miss the significance of this research if we don't acknowledge its strange intensity and exhilaration. What this work often involved was the experience of staring directly into the sun, of sunlight searing itself onto the body, palpably disturbing it into a proliferation of incandescent color. Clearly these scientists came to a piercing realization of the corporeality of vision. Not only did their work find the body to be the site and producer of chromatic events, but this discovery allowed them to conceive of an abstract optical experience, that is of a vision that did not represent or refer to objects in the world. And the work of all three, whether as technological invention or empirical scientific study, was directed toward the mechanization and formalization of vision.

Although not involved like Brewster or Plateau in the invention of any optical device, the career of Gustav Fechner is perhaps the most interesting when juxtaposed with Turner's.[9] Fechner confounds many of the conventional dichotomies on which much nineteenth-century intellectual history is

7.   The suggestion that Turner's suns are self-portraits is made in Paulson, "Turner's Graffiti: The Sun and Its Glosses," p. 182, and in Lindsay, *Turner,* p. 213.

8.   Turner's personal contact with Brewster is discussed in J. A. Fineberg, *The Life of J. M. W. Turner R.A.,* 2nd. ed. (Oxford, 1966), p. 277; Lindsay, *Turner,* p. 206; and Gerald E. Finely, "Turner's Colour and Optics: A New Route in 1822," *Journal of the Warburg and the Courtauld Institute* 36 (1973), p. 388.

9.   On Fechner's seminal position in the history of scientific psychology, see, for example, E. G. Boring, *A History of Experimental Psychology* (New York, 1950), pp. 275–296. For a general statement of his principles for the measurement of sensation, see Fechner, *Elements of Psychophysics,* trans. Helmut E. Adler, (New York, 1966), pp. 38–58; *Elemente der Psychophysik* (Leipzig, 1860), vol. 1, pp. 48–75.

founded. Standard accounts have insisted on a kind of split personality. On one hand he seemed a Romantic mystic immersed in the *Naturphilosophie* of Oken and Schelling and in a Spinozist pantheism.[10] On the other, he was the founder of a rigorously empirical and quantitative psychology, crucial for the later work of Wilhelm Wundt and Ernst Mach, providing them with the theoretical foundations for a comprehensive reduction of perceptual and psychic experience to measurable units. But these two dimensions of Fechner were always intertwined.[11] His exhilarating and finally agonizing experience of the sun in the late 1830s was no less primal than it was for Turner.[12] Already in 1825 a solar preoccupation infused Fechner's literary meditations on vision:

> Thus we may view our own eye as a creature of the sun on earth,
> a creature dwelling in and nourished by the sun's rays, and hence
> a creature structurally resembling its brothers on the sun. . . . But
> the sun's creatures, the higher beings I call angels, are eyes which
> have become autonomous, eyes of the highest inner development
> which retain nevertheless, the structure of the ideal eye. Light is
> their element as ours is air.[13]

This early declaration of an emanative, autonomous vision, of a luminous and radiant eye, is part of a wider recurrence in the nineteenth century of a Plotinian model of the observer to which Turner can also be linked.[14] In 1846

10.   On Fechner's "mystical" writings, see the "Introduction" by Walter Lowrie in *Religion of a Scientist: Selections from Gustav Theodor Fechner,* trans. and ed. Walter Lowrie (New York, 1946), pp. 9–81. See also Fechner, *Life After Death,* trans. Mary Wadsworth (New York, 1943). For Spinoza's relation to the work of Müller and Fechner, see Walter Bernard, "Spinoza's Influence on the Rise of Scientific Psychology," *Journal of the History of the Behavioral Sciences* 8 (April 1972), pp. 208–215.
11.   See, for example, William R. Woodward, "Fechner's Panpsychism: A Scientific Solution to the Mind-Body Problem," *Journal of the History of the Behavioral Sciences* 8 (October 1972), pp. 367–386.
12.   Fechner's so-called crisis of 1840–1843, his physical and mental problems resulting from his experiments with afterimages, is detailed by his nephew in Johannes Emil Kuntze, *Gustav Theodor Fechner: Ein deutsches Gelehrtenleben* (Leipzig, 1892), pp. 105–138. He also suffered severe eye strain due to the precise scalar readings needed for his studies of binocular vision.
13.   Gustav Fechner, "On the Comparative Anatomy of Angels," trans. Marilynn Marshall, *Journal of the History of the Behavioral Sciences* 5, no. 1 (1969), pp. 39–58.
14.   Goethe gave Plotinus a place of prominence in the introduction to his optics: "We are reminded here of . . . the words of an old mystic writer, which may be thus rendered,

Turner produced a painting titled *The Angel Standing in the Sun.* A square canvas exactly the size of *Light and Colour* of 1843, the formal structure here is also insistently circular. In both of them Turner's familiar vortex modulates into a pure spherical whirlpool of golden light: a radial conflation of eye and sun, of self and divinity, of subject and object.

In the center of the later work is the figure of a winged angel raising a sword. Turner's use of this symbol, however, is an indication less of his links to a Romantic or Miltonic tradition of such imagery than of his remoteness from the paradigm of the camera obscura. As it was for Fechner, the recourse to the angel, an object with no referent in the world, is a sign of the inadequacy of conventional means for representing the hallucinatory abstraction of his intense optical experiences. The angel becomes a symbolic acknowledgment by Turner of his own perceptual autonomy, an exalted announcement of the ungroundedness of vision. And it is in this sense that Turner's work can be said to be sublime: his painting is concerned with experience that transcends its possible representations, with the insufficiency of any object to his concept.[15]

But if Turner's work suggests the extent of experimentation and innovation in the articulation of new languages, effects, and forms made possible by the relative abstraction and autonomy of physiological perception, Fechner's epochal formalization of perceptual experience comes out of a related crisis of representation. Like Turner's art, Fechner's work is grounded in an

---

'If the eye were not sunny, how could we possibly perceive light? If God's own strength lived not in us, how could we delight in Divine things?' This immediate affinity between light and the eye will be denied by none . . . It will be more intelligible to assert that a dormant light resides in the eye, and that it may be excited by the slightest cause from within or without." *Theory of Colours,* p. liii. Heidegger discusses this passage from Goethe in his *Schelling's Treatise on the Essence of Human Freedom,* trans. Joan Stambaugh (Athens, Ohio, 1985), pp. 54–56. On Plotinus and his relation to the history of art theory, see Eric Alliez and Michel Feher, "Reflections of a Soul," *Zone* 4 (1989), pp. 46–84.

15.   My use of the term *sublime* refers to the work of Jean-François Lyotard, *The Postmodern Condition: A Report on Knowledge,* trans. Brian Massumi (Minneapolis, 1984), pp. 77–79: "Modernity in whatever age it appears, cannot exist without a shattering of belief and without discovery of the 'lack of reality' of reality, together with the invention of other realities. . . . I think in particular that it is in the aesthetic of the sublime that modern art (including literature) finds its impetus and the logic of avant-gardes its axioms. . . . The sentiment of the sublime . . . develops as a conflict between the faculties of a subject, the faculty to conceive of something and the faculty to 'present' something." See also Lyotard, "The Sublime and the Avant-Garde," *Artforum* 22 (April 1984), pp. 36–43.

J. M. W. Turner. The Angel Standing in the Sun. *1846.*

exhilaration and delirium made possible by the collapse of the dualities inherent in the camera obscura—its split between perceiver and world. Fechner had a primal certainty of the interconnection between mind and matter: they were simply alternate ways of construing the same reality. But what he wanted, and spent years seeking, was a method of establishing an exact relationship between interior sensory experience and events in the world, to situate these two domains on the same field of operations. Whatever his intentions, the end result was to relocate perception and the observer within the reach of empirical exactitude and technological intervention.

Sensation as a multiplicity of intangible psychic affects, however, was not in itself rationalizable—that is, it was not directly accessible to study, manipulation, duplication, and measurement as an empirically isolable entity. But if sensation did not lend itself to scientific control and management, any form of physical stimulus did. Thus Fechner set about rationalizing sensation through the measurement of external stimulus. Where Herbart had failed in his attempt at mental measurement, Fechner succeeded by quantifying sensations in terms of the stimuli that produced them. His achievement was the establishment of what is variously called Fechner's Law or Weber's Law, in which he proposed a mathematical equation that expressed a functional relation between sensation and stimulus.[16] With such an equation the inside/outside of the camera obscura dissolves and a new kind of annexation of the observer is made possible. For the first time subjectivity is made quantifiably determinable. This is Fechner's "Galilean" achievement—making measurable something that had not been so before.[17]

Fechner's research furthered the realization of the arbitrary or disjunctive relation of sensation to its external cause that Müller's work on nerve energies had already disclosed.[18] For example, he found that the intensity of

16.   Named for Ernst Weber, Fechner's teacher, whose work between 1838 and 1846 on the sense of touch was the basis for Fechner's proposals. Foucault cites Weber's work in the 1840s as coinciding with the emergence of a technology of behavior and the "supervision of normality" in a variety of fields. *Discipline and Punish*, pp. 294–296.
17.   See Harald Høffding, *History of Modern Philosophy*, vol. 2 (New York, 1955), p. 529: "The only difference between Fechner and Spinoza here is that Fechner is eager to discover a mathematical functional relation between the two sides of existence."
18.   "Even when applied in the same way, one and the same stimulus may be perceived as stronger or weaker by one subject or organ than by another, or by the same subject or

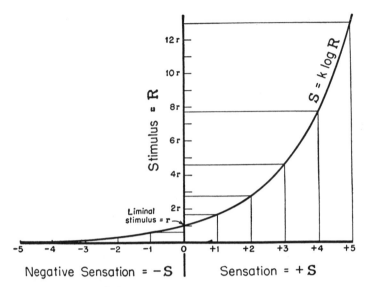

Fechner's Law: S = k *log* R.

a sensation of light does not increase as quickly as the intensity of the physical stimulus. Thus he concluded that there was a disproportional, though predictable, relation between increases in sensation and increases in stimulation. Central to Fechner's work was the establishment of measurable units of sensation, quantifiable increments that would allow human perception to be made calculable and productive. These were derived from thresholds of sensation, from the magnitude of the stimulus needed to generate the very least noticeable sensation over and above the stimulus that is unnoticed by the human sensorium. These units were the much-debated "just noticeable differences." Thus human perception became a sequence of magnitudes of varying intensity. As Fechner's experiments with afterimages also had shown him, perception was necessarily temporal; an observer's sensations always depended on the previous sequence of stimuli. But it is segmented temporality very different from that implied in Turner, or from the kind of experience that Bergson and others later sought to champion over the scientific project

---

organ at one time as stronger or weaker than at another. Conversely, stimuli of different magnitudes may be perceived as equally strong under certain circumstances." *Elements of Psychophysics,* p. 38.

initiated by Fechner. It is relevant that at the time Fechner was performing his experiments in the 1840s, George Boole was overlapping the operations of logic with those of algebra, attempting a related formalization of "the laws of thought." But as Foucault has insisted, mathematization or quantification, although important, is not the crucial issue in the human sciences in the nineteenth century.[19] Rather, at stake is how the human subject, through knowledge of the body and its modes of functioning, was made compatible with new arrangements of power: the body as worker, student, soldier, consumer, patient, criminal. Vision may well be measurable, but what is perhaps most significant about Fechner's equations is their homogenizing function: they are a means of rendering a perceiver manageable, predictable, productive, and above all consonant with other areas of rationalization.[20]

Fechner's formalization of perception renders the specific contents of vision irrelevant. Vision, as well as the other senses, is now describable in terms of abstract and exchangeable magnitudes. If vision previously had been conceived as an experience of *qualities* (as in Goethe's optics), it is now a question of differences in quantities, of sensory experience that is stronger or weaker. But this new valuation of perception, this obliteration of the qualitative in sensation through its arithmetical homogenization, is a crucial part of modernization.

19.   Michel Foucault, *The Order of Things,* pp. 349–351.
20.   "In a sense, the power of normalization imposes homogeneity; but it individualizes by making it possible to measure gaps, to determine levels, to fix specialties, and to render the differences useful by fitting them one to another. It is easy to understand how the power of the norm functions within a system of formal equality, since within a homogeneity that is the rule, the norm introduces, as a useful imperative and as a result of measurement, all the shading of individual differences." Michel Foucault, *Discipline and Punish,* p. 184. Foucault's notion of "homogeneity" recalls its place in the work of Georges Bataille: "*Homogeneity* signifies here the commensurability of elements and the awareness of this commensurability: human relations are sustained by a reduction to fixed rules based on the consciousness of the possible identity of delineable persons and situations. . . . The common denominator, the foundation of social homogeneity and of the activity arising from it, is money, namely the calculable equivalent of the different products of collective activity. Money serves to measure all work and makes man a function of measurable products. According to the judgment of *homogenous* society, each man is worth what he produces; in other words he stops being an existence for itself: he is no more than a function, arranged within measurable limits, of collective production (which makes him an existence for something other than itself.)" Bataille, *Visions of Excess: Selected Writings 1927–1939,* trans. Allan Stoekl (Minneapolis, 1985), pp. 137–138.

At the center of Fechner's psychophysics is the law of the conservation of energy, an insistence that organisms *and* inorganic nature are ruled by the same forces. He describes the human subject: "In a way the relations are like those of a steam engine with a complicated mechanism. . . . The only differences is that in our organic machine the engineer does not sit on the outside but on the inside."[21] And Fechner is certainly not alone here. All of Helmholtz's work on human vision, including binocular disparity, stemmed from his original interest in animal heat and respiration and his overriding ambition to describe the functioning of a living being in precise physiochemical terms. Thermodynamics stand behind both his and Fechner's delineation of a being that works, produces, and *sees* through a process of muscular exertion, combustion, and release of heat according to empirically verifiable laws.[22] Even if Fechner's dominant legacy is the hegemony of behaviorism and the myriad processes of conditioning and control, it is important to see how his psychophysics originally sought a delirious merging of the interiority of a perceiver into a single charged and unified field, every part of it vibrating with the same forces of repulsion and attraction, an infinite nature, like Turner's, where life and death are simply different states of a primal energy. But modern forms of power also arose through the dissolution of the boundaries that had kept the subject as an interior domain qualitatively separated from the world. Modernization demanded that this last retreat be rationalized, and as Foucault makes clear, all the sciences in the nineteenth century beginning with the prefix *psycho-* are part of this strategic appropriation of subjectivity.[23]

21.   Fechner, *Elements of Psychophysics,* p. 35.
22.   Fechner, *Elements of Psychophysics,* pp. 32–33: "Accordingly the kinetic energy of a system may increase without drawing on potential energy and may decrease without a corresponding increase of potential energy as long as the kinetic energy simultaneously decreases or increases in another part of the system . . . It is impossible to be lost in external perception and to think deeply at the same time. In order to reflect acutely on something we have to abstract from something else. . . . the facts are too closely connected with the previous discussion for us not to see also in them an extension of the law of the conservation of energy to the play of purely psychophysical forces."
23.   Foucault, *Discipline and Punish,* p. 193. Freud's expressed admiration for Fechner's "economic standpoint" is well known, but on a more general level psychoanalysis can be seen as another operation of relocating the "interior" contents of the unconscious onto a field where they can be formalized in linguistic terms, however imprecisely.

But Fechner's rationalization of sensation not only led to the development of specific technologies of behavior and attentiveness; it was also a sign of the reshaping of an entire social field and the position of a human sensorium within it. Later in the nineteenth century Georg Simmel found Fechner's formulations to be an incisive means of expressing how sensory experience had become adjacent and even coincident with an economic and cultural terrain dominated by exchange values. Simmel derived from Fechner an informal kind of calculation to demonstrate how exchange values were equivalent to quantities of physical stimulation. "Money," he wrote, "operates as a stimulus to all kinds of possible sentiments because its unspecific character, devoid of all qualities, places it at such a great distance from any sentiment that its relations with all of them are fairly equal."[24] In Simmel's account of modernity, the observer is conceivable only as an element in this flux and inexorable mobility of values: "Within the historical-psychological sphere, money by its very nature becomes the most perfect representative of a cognitive tendency of modern science as a whole—the reduction of qualitative determinations to quantitative ones."[25]

The "real world" that the camera obscura had stabilized for two centuries was no longer, to paraphrase Nietzsche, the most useful or valuable world. The modernity enveloping Turner, Fechner, and their heirs had no need of its kind of truth and immutable identities. A more adaptable, autonomous, and productive observer was needed in both discourse and practice—to conform to new functions of the body and to a vast proliferation of indifferent and convertible signs and images. Modernization effected a deterritorialization and a revaluation of vision.

In this book I have tried to give a sense of how radical was the reconfiguration of vision by the 1840s. If our problem is vision and modernity, we must first examine these earlier decades, not the modernist painting of the 1870s and 1880s. A new type of observer was formed then, and not one that

24.   Georg Simmel, *The Philosophy of Money,* trans. Tom Bottomore and David Frisby (London, 1978), p. 267. For Simmel's extended reconstrual of Fechner's Law, see pp. 262–271.
25.   Simmel, *The Philosophy of Money,* p. 277.

we can see figured in paintings or prints. We've been trained to assume that an observer will always leave visible tracks, that is, will be identifiable in relation to images. But here it's a question of an observer who also takes shape in other, grayer practices and discourses, and whose immense legacy will be all the industries of the image and the spectacle in the twentieth century. The body that had been a neutral or invisible term in vision was now the thickness from which knowledge of the observer was obtained. This palpable opacity and carnal density of vision loomed so suddenly into view that its full consequences and effects could not be immediately realized. But once vision became relocated in the subjectivity of the observer, two intertwined paths opened up. One led out toward all the multiple affirmations of the sovereignty and autonomy of vision derived from this newly empowered body, in modernism and elsewhere. The other path was toward the increasing standardization and regulation of the observer that issued from knowledge of visionary body, toward forms of power that depended on the abstraction and formalization of vision. What is important is how these paths continually intersect and often overlap on the same social terrain, amid the countless localities in which the diversity of concrete acts of vision occur.

Bibliography

•

Before 1900

Ampère, André-Marie. *Philosophie des deux Ampères.* Ed. J. Barthélemy-Saint-Hilaire. Paris: Didier, 1866.

Baudelaire, Charles. *Oeuvres Complètes.* Paris: Gallimard, 1961.

Bergson, Henri. *Matter and Memory.* [1896] Trans. W. S. Palmer and N. M. Paul. New York: Zone Books, 1988.

Berkeley, George. *The Works of George Berkeley, Bishop of Cloyne.* Ed. A. A. Luce and T. E. Jessop. London: Thomas Nelson, 1948.

Bichat, Xavier. *Recherches physiologiques sur la vie et la mort.* [1800] 3d. ed. Paris: Brosson, Gabon, 1805.

Blake, William. *Complete Writings.* Ed. Geoffrey Keynes. London: Oxford Univ. Press, 1966.

Brewster, Sir David. *Brewster and Wheatstone on Vision.* Ed. Nicholas J. Wade. London: Academic, 1983.

Brewster, Sir David. *The Kaleidoscope: Its History, Theory and Construction.* London: John Murray, 1858.

Brewster, Sir David. *Letters on Natural Magic.* New York: J. J. Harper, 1832.

Brewster, Sir David. *The Stereoscope: Its History, Theory and Construction with Its Application to the Fine and Useful Arts and to Education.* London: John Murray, 1856.

Condillac, Etienne. *Oeuvres philosophiques de Condillac.* Ed. Georges LeRoy. Paris: Presses Universitaires de France, 1947–1951.

Descartes, René. *Oeuvres philosophiques.* Ed. Ferdinand Alquié. 3 vols. Paris: Garnier, 1963–73.

Descartes, René. *The Philosophical Writings of Descartes.* 2 vols. Trans. John Cottingham, Robert Stoothoff, & Dugald Murdoch. Cambridge: Cambridge Univ. Press, 1985.

Diderot, Denis. *Oeuvres esthètiques.* Ed. Paul Vernière. Paris: Garnier, 1968.

Diderot, Denis. *Oeuvres philosophiques.* Ed. Paul Vernière. Paris: Garnier, 1964.

Encyclopédie ou Dictionnaire raisonné des sciences, des arts et des métiers. Paris, 1750–70.

Engels, Friedrich, and Karl Marx. *The German Ideology.* Ed. R. Pascal. New York: International, 1947.

Fechner, Gustav Theodor. *Elemente der Psychophysik.* 2 vols. Leipzig: Breitkopf & Härtel, 1860.

Fechner, Gustav Theodor. *Elements of Psychophysics.* Trans. Helmut E. Adler. Ed. Davis H. Howes. New York: Holt, Rinehart and Winston, 1966.

Fechner, Gustav Theodor. *Life After Death.* Trans. Mary C. Wadsworth and Eugene Jolas. New York: Pantheon, 1943.

Fechner, Gustav Theodor. *Religion of a Scientist: Selections From Gustav Th. Fechner.* Trans. and ed. Walter Lowrie. New York: Pantheon, 1946.

Flourens, Pierre. *Recherches expérimentales sur les propriétés et les fonctions du système nerveux dans les animaux vertébrés.* Paris: Crouvost, 1824.

Freud, Sigmund. *The Interpretation of Dreams.* [1899] Trans. James Strachey. New York: Basic Books, 1955.

Goethe, Johann Wolfgang von. *Gedenkausgabe der Werke, Briefe, und Gesprache.* Ed. Ernst Beutler. Zurich, 1949.

Goethe, Johann Wolfgang von. *Theory of Colours.* Trans. Charles Eastlake [1840]. Cambridge, Mass. MIT Press, 1970.

Hall, Marshall. *Memoirs on the Nervous System.* London: Sherwood, Gilbert and Piper. 1837.

Harris, John. *Lexicon Technicum: or a Universal English Dictionary of Arts and Sciences.* London: D. Brown, 1704.

Harris, Joseph. *A Treatise of Optics: Containing Elements of the Science.* London: B. White, 1775.

Hegel, G. W. F. *The Phenomenology of Mind.* Trans. J. B. Baillie. New York: Harper and Row, 1967.

Helmholtz, Hermann von. *Handbook of Physiological Optics.* 3 vols. Trans. George T. Ladd. New York: Dover, 1962.

Helmholtz, Hermann von. *On the Sensation of Tone.* Trans. Alexander Ellis. New York: Dover, 1954.

Helmholtz, Hermann von. *Popular Scientific Lectures.* Ed. Morris Kline. New York: Dover, 1962.

Herbart, Johann Friedrich. *Psychologie als Wissenschaft.* 2 vols. Königsberg: August Unzer, 1825.

Herbart, Johann Friedrich. *A Textbook in Psychology: An Attempt to Found the Science of Psychology on Experience, Metaphysics and Mathematics.* Trans. Margaret K. Smith. New York: Appleton, 1891.

Hobbes, Thomas. *Leviathan.* Ed. Michael Oakeshott. Oxford: Basil Blackwell, 1957.

Holmes, Oliver Wendell. "The Stereoscope and the Stereograph." *Atlantic Monthly* 3, no. 20 (June 1859), pp. 738–748.

Hume, David. *An Inquiry Concerning Human Understanding.* Ed. Charles Hendel. Indianapolis: Bobbs-Merrill, 1955.

Hutton, Charles. *A Mathematical and Philosophical Dictionary.* 2 vols. London: J. Davis, 1796.

Janet, Paul. "Schopenhauer et la physiologie française: Cabanis et Bichat," *Revue des deux mondes* 39 (1880), pp. 35–39.

Jombert, Charles-Antoine. *Méthode pour apprendre le dessein.* Paris, 1755.

Kant, Immanuel. *Critique of Judgement.* Trans. J. H. Bernard. New York: Hafner, 1951.

Kant, Immanuel. *Critique of Pure Reason.* Trans. Norman Kemp Smith. New York: St. Martin's, 1965.

Kircher, Athanasius. *Ars magna lucis et umbrae.* Rome, 1646.

Kuntze, Johannes Emil. *Gustav Fechner: Ein deutsches Gelehrtenleben.* Leipzig: Breitkopf & Härtel, 1892.

Leibniz, Gottfried Wilhelm von. *Monadology and Other Philosophical Essays.* Trans. Paul Schrecker and Anne Martin Schrecker. Indianapolis: Bobbs-Merrill, 1965.

Leibniz, Gottfried Wilhelm von. *New Essays on Human Understanding.* Trans. Peter Remnant and Jonathan Bennett. Cambridge: Cambridge Univ. Press, 1981.

Locke, John. *An Essay Concerning Human Understanding.* Ed. Alexander Campbell Fraser. 2 vols. 1894. Rpt. New York: Dover, 1959.

Mach, Ernst. *Contributions to the Analysis of Sensations.* [1885] Trans. C. M. Williams. La Salle, Ill.: Open Court, 1890.

Maine de Biran. "Considérations sur les principes d'une division des faits psychologiques et physiologiques." In *Oeuvres de Maine de Biran,* vol. 13, ed. P. Tisserand. Paris: Presses Universitaires de France, 1949.

Maine de Biran. *Influence de l'habitude sur la faculté de penser.* Ed. P. Tisserand. Paris: Presses Universitaires de France, 1953.

Marx, Karl. *Capital.* 3 vols. Trans. Samuel Moore and Edward Aveling. New York: International, 1967.

Marx, Karl. *Economic and Philosophical Manuscripts of 1844.* Trans. Martin Milligan. New York: International, 1968.

Marx, Karl. *Grundrisse.* Trans. Martin Nicolaus. New York: Random House, 1973.

Molyneux, William. *Dioptrica nova. A treatise of dioptricks, in two parts.* London: B. Tooke, 1692.

Müller, Johannes. *Elements of Physiology.* 2 vols. Trans. William Baly. London: Taylor and Walton, 1848.

Müller, Johannes. *Handbuch des Physiologie des Menschen.* Coblenz: J. Hölscher, 1838.

Müller, Johannes. *Zur vergleichenden Physiologie des Gesichtssinnes.* Leipzig: C. Cnobloch, 1826.

Newton, Sir Isaac. *Opticks, or a Treatise of the Reflections, Refractions, Inflections and Colours of Light.* 4th ed. London, 1730. Rpt. New York: Dover, 1952.

Nietzsche, Friedrich. *Genealogy of Morals.* Trans. Walter Kaufmann, New York: Random House, 1968.

Nietzsche, Friedrich. *Human, All Too Human.* Trans. R. J. Hollingdale. Cambridge: Cambridge Univ. Press, 1986.

Nietzsche, Friedrich. *The Will To Power.* Trans. Walter Kaufmann and R. J. Hollingdale. New York: Random House, 1968.

Paris, John A. *Philosophy in Sport Made Science in Earnest, Being an Attempt to Illustrate the first principles of Natural Philosophy by the Aid of the Popular Toys and Sports.* Vol. 3. London: Thornburn, 1827.

Porta, Giambattista della. *Natural Magick.* London: Young and Speed, 1658. Originally published as *Magiae naturalis.* Naples, 1558.

Porterfield, William. *A Treatise on the Eye, the Manner and Phenomena of Vision.* Edinburgh: Hamilton and Balfour, 1759.

Purkinje, Jan. "Visual Phenomena." Trans. H. R. John. In *History of Psychology: A Source Book in Systematic Psychology,* ed. William Sahakian. Itasca, Ill.: F. E. Peacock, 1968.

Reid, Thomas. *Essays on the Powers of the Human Mind.* 3 vols. Edinburgh: Bell & Bradfute, 1819.

Ribot, Théodule. *La psychologie d'attention*. Paris: F. Alcan, 1889.

Roget, Peter Mark. "Explanations of an optical deception in the appearance of the spokes of a wheel . . ." *Philosophical Transactions of the Royal Society* 115 (1825), pp. 131–140.

Ruskin, John. *The Works of John Ruskin*. Ed. E. T. Cook. London: George Allen, 1903–1912.

Schelling, F. W. J. *The Ages of the World*. Trans. Fredrick de Wolfe Bolman. New York: Columbia Univ. Press, 1942.

Schopenhauer, Arthur. *Parerga and Paralipomena*. Trans. E. F. J. Payne. 2 vols. Oxford: Clarendon, 1974.

Schopenhauer, Arthur. *Sämtliche Werke*. 16 vols. Ed. Paul Deussen. Munich: Piper, 1911–42.

Schopenhauer, Arthur. *Textes sur la vue et sur les couleurs*. Trans. Maurice Elie. Paris: J. Vrin, 1986.

Schopenhauer, Arthur. *The World as Will and Representation*. 2 vols. Trans. E. F. J. Payne. New York: Dover, 1958.

The Spectator. Ed. Donald F. Bond. 5 vols. Oxford: Oxford Univ. Press, 1965.

Wheatstone, Charles. *Brewster and Wheatstone on Vision*. Ed. Nicholas J. Wade. London: Academic, 1983.

After 1900

Abrams, M. H. *The Mirror and the Lamp: Romantic Theory and the Critical Tradition*. London: Oxford Univ. Press, 1953.

Adorno, Theodor. *Aesthetic Theory*. Trans. C. Leenhardt. London: RKP, 1984.

Adorno, Theodor. *In Search of Wagner*. Trans. Rodney Livingstone. London: Verso, 1981.

Adorno, Theodor. *Minima Moralia*. Trans. Edmund Jephcott. London: Verso, 1974.

Alliez, Eric, and Michel Feher. "Reflections of a Soul." *Zone* 4, (1989), pp. 46–84.

Alpers, Svetlana. *The Art of Describing: Dutch Art in the Seventeenth Century*. Chicago: Univ. of Chicago Press, 1983.

Alpers, Svetlana. *Rembrandt's Enterprise: The Studio and the Market*. Chicago: Univ. of Chicago Press, 1988.

Anderson, Barbara and Joseph. "Motion Perception in Motion Pictures." In *The Cinematic Apparatus,* ed. Teresa de Lauretis. London: Macmillan, 1980, pp. 76–95.

Aumont, Jacques. "Le point de vue." *Communications* 38 (1983), pp. 3–29.

Barker, Francis. *The Tremulous Private Body: Essays on Subjection*. New York: Methuen, 1984.

Barnes, John. *Precursors of the Cinema: Peepshows, Panoramas and Dioramas*. St. Ives, Cornwall: Barnes Museum of Cinematography, 1967.

Barnouw, Erik. *The Magician and the Cinema*. Oxford: Oxford Univ. Press, 1981.

Barthes, Roland. *Camera Lucida*. Trans. Richard Howard. New York: Hill and Wang, 1981.

Barthes, Roland. *Image-Music-Text*. Trans. Stephen Heath. New York: Hill and Wang, 1977.

Barthes, Roland. *The Rustle of Language*. Trans. Richard Howard. New York: Hill and Wang, 1986.

Bataille, Georges. *Visions of Excess: Selected Writings 1927–1939*. Trans. Alan Stoekl. Minneapolis: Univ. of Minnesota, 1985.

Baudrillard, Jean. *La societé de consommation*. Paris: Gallimard, 1970.

Baudrillard, Jean. *Pour une critique de l'économie politique du signe.* Paris: Gallimard, 1972.

Baudrillard, Jean. *Simulations.* New York: Semiotexte, 1983.

Baudry, Jean. "Ideological Effects of the Basic Cinematographic Apparatus." In *Apparatus,* ed. Theresa Hak Kyung Cha. New York: Tanam, 1980.

Benjamin, Walter. *Charles Baudelaire: A Lyric Poet in the Era of High Capitalism.* Trans. Harry Zohn. London: NLB, 1973.

Benjamin, Walter. *Illuminations.* Trans. Harry Zohn. New York: Schocken, 1969.

Benjamin, Walter. *One Way Street.* Trans. Edmund Jephcott and Kingsley Shorter. London: NLB, 1979.

Benjamin, Walter. *Das Passagen-Werk,* 2 vols. Frankfurt: Suhrkamp, 1982.

Benjamin, Walter. *Reflections.* Trans. Edmund Jephcott. New York: Harcourt Brace Jovanovich, 1979.

Bergson, Henri. *Creative Evolution.* [1907] Trans. Arthur Mitchell. New York, Random House, 1944.

Bernal, J. D. *Science in History.* Vol. 2 *The Scientific and Industrial Revolutions.* 1954. Rpt. Cambridge, Mass.: MIT Press, 1971.

Bernard, Walter. "Spinoza's Influence on the Rise of Scientific Psychology." *Journal of the History of the Behavioral Sciences* 8 (April 1972), pp. 208–215.

Blumenberg, Hans. *Legitimacy of the Modern Age.* Trans. Robert M. Wallace. Cambridge, Mass.: MIT Press, 1983.

Boring, Edwin G. *A History of Experimental Psychology.* New York: Appleton-Century-Crofts, 1950.

Bryson, Norman. *Word and Image: French Painting of the Ancien Regime.* Cambridge: Cambridge Univ. Press, 1981.

Buchwald, Jed Z. *The Rise of the Wave Theory of Light: Optical Theory and Experiment in the Early Nineteenth Century.* Chicago: Univ. of Chicago Press, 1989.

Buck-Morss, Susan. "The Flaneur, The Sandwichman, and the Whore: The Politics of Loitering." *New German Critique* 39 (Fall 1986), pp. 99–140.

Buddemier, Heinz. *Panorama, Diorama, Photographie: Entstehung und Wirkung neuer Medien im 19. Jahrhundert.* Munich: H. Fink, 1970.

Burch, Noel. "Charles Baudelaire versus Doctor Frankenstein." *Afterimage* 8–9 (Spring 1981), pp. 4–23.

Canguilhem, Georges. *Etudes d'histoire et de philosophie des sciences.* Paris: J. Vrin, 1983.

Canguilhem, Georges. *The Normal and the Pathological.* Trans. Carolyn R. Fawcett. New York: Zone Books, 1989.

Cantor, G. N. *Optics After Newton.* Manchester: Manchester Univ. Press, 1983.

Cassirer, Ernst. *The Individual and the Cosmos in Renaissance Philosophy.* Trans. Mario Domandi. Philadelphia: Univ. of Pennsylvania Press, 1972.

Cassirer, Ernst. *The Philosophy of the Enlightenment.* [1932] Trans. Fritz C. A. Koelln and James P. Petlegrove. Princeton: Princeton Univ. Press, 1951.

Cassirer, Ernst. *Rousseau, Kant, and Goethe.* Trans. James Gutman, John Herman Randall, Jr., and Paul Oskar Kristeller. Princeton: Princeton Univ. Press, 1945.

Castle, Terry. "Phantasmagoria: Spectral Technology and the Metaphorics of Modern Reverie." *Critical Inquiry* 15 (Autumn 1988), pp. 26–61.

Ceram, C. W. *Archaeology of the Cinema.* New York: Harcourt, Brace and World, 1965.

Chanan, Michael. *The Dream that Kicks: The Prehistory and Early Years of Cinema in Brit-ain.* London: Routledge and Kegan Paul, 1980.

Changeux, Jean-Pierre. *Neuronal Man: The Biology of Mind.* Trans. Lawrence Garey. New York: Oxford Univ. Press, 1985.

Clark, T. J. *The Painting of Modern Life: Paris in the Art of Manet and His Followers.* Prince-ton: Princeton Univ. Press, 1984.

Clarke, Edwin, and L. S. Jacyna. *Nineteenth Century Origins of Neuroscientific Concepts.* Berkeley: Univ. of California Press, 1987.

Comolli, Jean-Louis. "Machines of the Visible." In *The Cinematic Apparatus,* ed. Teresa de Lauretis. London: Macmillan, 1980.

Comolli, Jean-Louis. "Technique et idéologie." *Cahiers du cinéma* 229 (May–June 1971), pp. 4–21.

Constable, W. G., and J. G. Links. *Canaletto.* 2 vols. Oxford: Clarendon, 1976.

Corboz, André. *Canaletto: Una Venezia immaginaria.* 2 vols. Milan: Electra, 1985.

Crary, Jonathan. "Eclipse of the Spectacle." In *Art After Modernism: Rethinking Represen-tation,* ed. Brian Wallis. Boston: David Godine, 1984, pp. 283–294.

Crary, Jonathan. "Spectacle, Attention, Counter-Memory." *October* 50, (Fall 1988). pp. 97–107.

Damisch, Hubert. *L'origine de la perspective.* Paris: Flammarion, 1988.

Danto, Arthur. "The Representational Character of Ideas and the Problem of the External World." In *Descartes: Critical and Interpretive Essays,* ed. Michael Hooker. Balti-more: John Hopkins Univ. Press, 1978.

Debord, Guy. *The Society of the Spectacle.* Trans. Donald Nicholson-Smith. New York: Swerve Editions, 1990.

De Landa, Manuel. *War in the Age of Intelligent Machines.* New York: Zone Books, 1990.

Deleule, Didier, and François Guéry. *Le corps productif.* Paris: Mame, 1972.

Deleuze, Gilles. *Cinema 1: The Movement-Image.* Trans. Hugh Tomlinson and Barbara Habberjam. Minneapolis: Univ. of Minnesota Press, 1986.

Deleuze, Gilles. *Foucault.* Trans. Seán Hand. Minneapolis: University of Minnesota Press, 1988.

Deleuze, Gilles. *Le pli: Leibniz et le baroque.* Paris: Minuit, 1988.

Deleuze, Gilles, and Félix Guattari. *Anti-Oedipus.* Trans. Mark Seem, Robert Hurley, and Helen Lane. New York: Viking, 1978.

Deleuze, Gilles, and Félix Guattari. *A Thousand Plateaus.* Trans. Brian Massumi. Minne-apolis: Univ. of Minnesota Press, 1987.

de Man, Paul. *Blindness and Insight: Essays in the Rhetoric of Contemporary Criticism.* New York: Oxford Univ. Press, 1974.

Dijksterhuis, E. J., ed. *Descartes et le cartésianism hollandais: Etudes et documents.* Paris: Presses Universitaires de France, 1950.

Dreyfus, Hubert, and Paul Rabinow. *Michel Foucault: Beyond Hermeneutics and Struc-turalism.* Chicago: Univ. of Chicago Press, 1982.

Dunkel, Harold B. *Herbart and Herbartism: An Educational Ghost Story.* Chicago: Univ. of Chicago Press, 1970.

Earle, Edward W. *Points of View: The Stereoscope in America: A Cultural History.* Rochester: Visual Studies Workshop, 1979.

Eder, Josef Maira. *History of Photography.* Trans. Edward Epstein. New York: Dover, 1945. Rpt. of 4th edition, 1932.

Escoubas, Eliane, "L'oeil (du) teinturier." *Critique* 37, no. 418 (March 1982), pp. 231–242.

Feyerabend, Paul. *Against Method.* London: Verso, 1975.

Feyerabend, Paul. *Problems of Empiricism.* 2 vols. Cambridge: Cambridge Univ. Press, 1981.

Fineberg, J. A. *The Life of J. M. W. Turner R.A.* 2nd. ed. Oxford: Oxford Univ. Press, 1966.

Fink, Daniel A. "Vermeer's Use of Camera Obscura: A Comparative Study." *Art Bulletin* 53 no. 4 (December 1971), pp. 493–505.

Finley, Gerald E. "Turner: An Early Experiment with Colour Theory." *Journal of the Warburg and Courtauld Institute* 30 (1967), pp. 357–366.

Finley, Gerald E. "Turner's Colour and Optics: A New Route in 1822." *Journal of the Warburg and Courtauld Institute* 36 (1973), pp. 385–390.

Fontenay, Elisabeth de. *Diderot: Reason and Resonance.* Trans. Jeffrey Mehlman. New York: Braziller, 1982.

Forbes, Eric G. "Goethe's Vision of Science." In *Common Denominators in Art and Science,* ed. Martin Pollock. Aberdeen: Aberdeen Univ. Press, 1983, pp. 9–15.

Foucault, Michel. *The Birth of the Clinic: An Archaeology of Medical Perception.* Trans. A. M. Sheridan Smith. New York: Pantheon, 1975.

Foucault, Michel. *Discipline and Punish: The Birth of the Prison.* Trans. Alan Sheridan. New York: Pantheon, 1979.

Foucault, Michel. *Madness and Civilization: A History of Insanity in the Age of Reason.* Trans. Richard Howard. New York: Pantheon, 1973.

Foucault, Michel. *The Order of Things.* New York: Pantheon, 1973.

Foucault, Michel. *Power/Knowledge: Selected Interviews and Other Writings 1972–1977.* Ed. Colin Gordon. New York: Pantheon, 1980.

Frankel, Edward. "Corpuscular Optics and the Wave Theory of Light: The Science and Politics of a Revolution in Physics." *Social Studies of Science* 6 (1976), pp. 141–184.

Fried, Michael. *Absorption and Theatricality: Painting and Beholder in the Age of Diderot.* Berkeley: Univ. of California Press, 1980.

Fritzsche, Hellmuth Allwill. *Bernardo Belotto genannt Canaletto.* Magdeburg: August Hopfer, 1936.

Gage, John. "Turner's Annotated Books: Goethe's 'Theory of Colour.'" *Turner Studies* 4 (Winter 1982), pp. 34–52.

Garin, Eugenio. *Italian Humanism: Philosophy and Civic Life in the Renaissance.* Trans. Peter Munz. New York: Harper and Row, 1965.

Gearhart, Suzanne. *Open Boundary of History and Fiction: A Critical Approach to the French Enlightenment.* Princeton: Princeton Univ. Press, 1984.

Gerlach, Joachim. "Über neurologische Erkenntniskritik." *Schopenhauer-Jahrbuch* 53 (1972), pp. 393–401.

Gernsheim, Helmut and Alison. *The History of Photography.* 2nd. ed. London: Thames and Hudson, 1969.

Gernsheim, Helmut and Alison. *L. J. M. Daguerre: The History of the Diorama and the Daguerreotype.* New York: Dover, 1968.

Gill, A. T. "Early Stereoscopes." *The Photographic Journal.* 109 (1969), pp. 546–599, 606–614, 641–651.

Gioseffi, Decio. *Canaletto: Il quaderno delle Gallerie Veneziane e l'impiego della camera ottica.* Instituto de Storia dell' Arte Antica e Moderna, no. 91, Univ. of Trieste 1959.

Gliozzi, Mario. "L'invenzione della camera oscura." *Archivo di Storia Della Scienza* vol. xiv, no. 2 (April–June 1932), pp. 221–229.

Gowing, Lawrence. *Turner: Imagination and Reality.* New York: Museum of Modern Art, 1966.

Gowing, Lawrence. *Vermeer.* 1952. Rpt. New York: Harper and Row, 1970.

Gregory, R. L. *Eye and Brain: The Psychology of Seeing.* 3d. ed. New York: McGraw-Hill, 1979.

Guillaume, Marc. *Eloge du désordre.* Paris: Gallimard, 1978.

Hacaen, Henri, and G. Lanteri-Laura. *Evolutions des connaissances et des doctrines sur les localisations cérébrales.* Paris: Desclée de Brouwer, 1977.

Hacking, Ian. *Representing and Intervening: Introductory Topics in Scientific Tradition and Change.* Chicago: Univ. of Chicago Press, 1979.

Haigh, Elizabeth Luckha. *Xavier Bichat and the Medical Theory of the Eighteenth Century.* London: Wellcome Institute for the History of Medicine, 1984.

Hallyn, Fernand. *The Poetic Structure of the World: Copernicus and Kepler.* Trans. Donald Leslie. New York: Zone Books, 1990.

Harman, P. M. *Energy, Force, and Matter: The Conceptual Development of Nineteenth-Century Physics.* Cambridge: Cambridge Univ. Press, 1982.

Harries, Karsten. "Descartes, Perspective and the Angelic Eye." *Yale French Studies* 49, (1973), pp. 28–42.

Heidegger, Martin. *The Question Concerning Technology and Other Essays.* Trans. William Lovitt. New York: Harper and Row, 1977.

Heidegger, Martin. *Schelling's Treatise on the Essence of Human Freedom.* Trans. Joan Stambaugh. Athens,Ohio: Ohio Univ. Press, 1985.

Henry, Michel. *Philosophie et phénoménologie du corps: essai sur l'ontologie biranienne.* Paris: Presses Universitaires de France, 1965.

Hess, Gunter, "Panorama und Denkmal: Erinnerung als Denkform Zwischen Vormarz und Grunderzeit." In *Literatur in der sozialen Bewegung: Aufsatze und Forschungsberichte zum 19. Jahrhundert,* ed. Gunter Hantzschel and George Jager. Tubingen: Max Niemeyer, 1977.

Høffding, Harald. *History of Modern Philosophy.* 2 vols. New York: Macmillan, 1955.

Horkheimer, Max, and Theodor Adorno. *Dialectic of Enlightenment.* Trans. John Cumming. New York: Seabury, 1972.

Husserl, Edmund. *The Crisis of European Science and Transcendental Phenomenology.* Trans. David Carr. Evanston: Northwestern Univ. Press, 1970.

Huxley, Aldous. *Themes and Variations.* London: Chatto and Windus, 1950.

Huyssen, Andreas. *After the Great Divide: Modernism, Mass Culture, Postmodernism.* Bloomington: Univ. of Indiana Press, 1986.

Irigaray, Luce. *Speculum of the Other Woman.* Trans. Gillian C. Gill. Ithaca: Cornell Univ. Press, 1985.

Jameson, Fredric. *The Ideologies of History: Essays 1971–1986.* 2 vols. Minneapolis: Univ. of Minnesota Press, 1988.

Jameson, Fredric. *The Political Unconscious: Narrative as a Socially Symbolic Act.* Ithaca: Cornell Univ. Press, 1981.

Jay, Martin. "Scopic Regimes of Modernity." In *Vision and Visuality,* ed. Hal Foster. Seattle: Bay Press, 1988.

Junod, Phillipe. *Transparence et opacité: Essai sur les fondaments théoriques de l'art moderne.* Lausanne: L'Age d'Homme, 1975.

Kofman, Sarah. *Camera obscura de l'idéologie.* Paris: Galilée, 1973.

Köller, Gottfried. *Das Leben des Biologen Johannes Müller.* Stuttgart: Wissenschaftliche Verlagsgesellschaft, 1958.

Krauss, Rosalind. "Antivision." *October* 36 (Spring 1986), pp. 147–154.

Krauss, Rosalind. "The Blink of an Eye," In *The States of Theory: History, Art, and Critical Discourse,* ed. David Caroll. New York: Columbia Univ. Press, 1990.

Krauss, Rosalind. "The Impulse to See." In *Vision and Visuality,* ed. Hal Foster. Seattle: Bay Press, 1988.

Krauss, Rosalind. "Photography's Discursive Spaces: Landscape/View." *Art Journal* 42, no. 4 (Winter 1982), pp. 311–319.

Kroeber, Karl. "Romantic Historicism: The Temporal Sublime." In *Images of Romanticism: Verbal and Visual Affinities,* ed. Karl Kroeber and William Walling. New Haven: Yale Univ. Press. 1978.

Kuhn, Thomas S. *The Essential Tension: Selected Studies in Scientific Tradition and Change.* Chicago: Univ. of Chicago Press, 1977.

Kuhn, Thomas S. *The Structure of Scientific Revolutions.* 2nd ed. Chicago: Univ. of Chicago Press, 1970.

Kuyper, Eric de, and Emile Poppe. "Voir et regarder." *Communications* 34 (1981), pp. 85–96.

Lacan, Jacques. *The Four Fundamental Concepts of Psycho-Analysis.* Trans. Alan Sheridan. New York: Norton, 1978.

Lauxtermann, P. F. H. "Five Decisive Years: Schopenhauer's Epistemology as Reflected in his Theory of Color." *Studies in the History and Philosophy of Science* 18, no. 3 (1987), pp. 271–291.

Leary, David, E. "The Historical Foundations of Herbart's Mathematization of Psychology." *Journal of the History of the Behavioral Sciences* 16, (1980), pp. 150–163.

Leary, David E. "The Philosophical Development of the Conception of Psychology in Germany, 1780–1850." *Journal of the History of the Behavioral Sciences* 14 (1978), pp. 113–121.

Leclerc, Hélène. "La scène d'illusion et l'hégémonie du théâtre à l'italienne." In *Histoire des spectacles,* ed. Guy Dumur. Paris: Gallimard, 1965, pp. 581–624.

Lenoble, Robert. *Histoire de l'idée de nature.* Paris: Editions Michel Albin, 1969.

Lindberg, David C. *Theories of Vision from Al-Kindi to Kepler.* Chicago: Univ. of Chicago Press, 1976.

Lindsay, Jack. *Turner: His Life and Work.* New York: Harper and Row, 1966.

Löwith, Karl. *From Hegel to Nietzsche: The Revolution in Nineteenth-Century Thought.* Trans. David E. Green. New York: Holt, Rinehart and Winston, 1964.

Lukács, Georg. *History and Class Consciousness.* Trans. Rodney Livingstone. Cambridge, Mass.: MIT Press, 1971.

Lyotard, Jean-François. *Discours, Figure.* Paris: Klincksieck, 1978.

Lyotard, Jean-François. *The Postmodern Condition: A Report on Knowledge.* Trans. Geoff Bennington and Brian Massumi. Minneapolis: Univ. of Minnesota Press, 1984.

Lyotard, Jean-François. "The Sublime and the Avant-Garde." *Artforum* 22, (April 1984), pp. 36–43.

Magnus, Rudolf. *Goethe as a Scientist.* 1906. Trans. Heinz Norden. New York: Henry Schuman, 1949.

Mandelbaum, Maurice. *History, Man, and Reason: A Study in Nineteenth-Century Thought.* Baltimore: Johns Hopkins Univ. Press, 1971.

Mandelbaum, Maurice. "The Physiological Orientation of Schopenhauer's Epistemology." In *Schopenhauer: His Philosophical Achievement,* ed. Michael Fox. Sussex: Harvester, 1980.

Marin, Louis. *Portrait of the King.* Trans. Martha Houle, Minneapolis: Univ. of Minnesota Press, 1988.

Markovits, Francine. "Diderot, Mérian, et l'aveugle." In J.B. Mérian, *Sur le problème de Molyneux.* Paris: Flammarion, 1984.

Mayor, A. Hyatt. "The Photographic Eye." *Metropolitan Museum of Art Bulletin* 5, no. 1 (Summer 1946), pp. 15–26.

Mehlman, Jeffrey. *Cataract: A Study in Diderot.* Middletown, Conn.: Weselyan Univ. Press, 1979.

Meredieu, Florence de. "De l'obscenité photographique." *Traverses* 29 (1983), pp. 86–94.

Merleau-Ponty, Maurice. *The Primacy of Perception.* Ed. James M. Edie. Evansville, Ill.: Northwestern Univ. Press, 1964.

Metz, Christian. *Film Language.* Trans. Michael Taylor. New York: Oxford Univ. Press, 1974.

Meyerson, Emile. *Identity and Reality.* Trans. Kate Lowenberg. New York: Dover, 1962.

Mitchell, W. J. T. *Iconology: Image, Text, Ideology.* Chicago: Univ. of Chicago Press, 1986.

Mitry, Jean. *Histoire du cinéma.* 2 vols. Paris: Editions Universitaires, 1967.

Morgan, M. J. *Molyneux's Question: Vision, Touch and the Philosophy of Perception.* Cambridge: Cambridge Univ. Press, 1977.

Neale, Steve. *Cinema and Technology: Image, Sound, Colour.* Bloomington: Indiana Univ. Press, 1985.

Neite, W. "The Cologne Diorama." *History of Photography* 3 (April 1979), pp. 105–109.

Nichols, Bill, and Susan J. Lederman. "Flicker and Motion in Film." In *The Cinematic Apparatus,* ed. Teresa de Lauretis and Stephen Heath. London: Macmillan, 1980, pp. 96–105.

Nisbet, H. B. *Goethe and the Scientific Tradition.* London: Univ. of London Press, 1972.

Oettermann, Stephen. *Das Panorama.* Munich: Syndikat, 1980.

Ostwald, Wilhelm. *Goethe, Schopenhauer, und die Farbenlehre.* Leipzig: Verlag Unesma, 1931.

Panofsky, Erwin. "Die Perspektive als 'Symbolische Form.'" *Vortrage der Bibliothek Warburg* (1924–25), pp. 258–330.

Paulson, Ronald. "Turner's Graffiti: The Sun and Its Glosses." In *Images of Romanticism: Verbal and Visual Affinities,* ed. Karl Kroeber and William Walling. New Haven: Yale Univ. Press, 1978.

Petrysak, Nicholas G. "Tabula Rasa: Its Origins and Implications." *Journal of the History of the Behavioral Sciences* 17 (1981), pp. 15–27.

Podro, Michael. *The Critical Historians of Art.* New Haven: Yale Univ. Press, 1982.

Podro, Michael. *The Manifold in Perception: Theories of Art from Kant to Hildebrand.* Oxford: Oxford Univ. Press, 1972.

Pomian, Krzysztof. *L'ordre du temps.* Paris: Gallimard, 1984.

Prigogine, Ilya, and Isabelle Stengers. *Order Out of Chaos.* New York: Bantam, 1984.

Quigley, Martin. *Magic Shadows: The Story of the Origin of Motion Pictures.* Washington, D.C.: Georgetown Univ. Press, 1948.

Quintavalle, Arturo. "The Philosophical Context of Riegl's 'Stilfragen.'" in *On the Methodology of Architectural History,* ed. Demetri Porphyrios. New York: St. Martin's, 1981.

Rabinow, Paul. *French Modern: Norms and Forms of the Social Environment.* Cambridge, Mass.: MIT Press, 1989.

Rajchman, John. "Foucault's Art of Seeing." *October* 44 (Spring 1988), pp. 89–117.

Reiss, Timothy J. *The Discourse of Modernism.* Ithaca, N.Y.: Cornell Univ. Press, 1982.

Ricoeur, Paul, *The Conflict of Interpretations.* Trans. Don Idhe. Evanston: Northwestern Univ. Press, 1974.

Rienstra, Miller H. "Giovanni Battista della Porta and Renaissance Science." Ph.D. diss., Univ. of Michigan, 1963.

Rorty, Richard. *Philosophy and the Mirror of Nature.* Princeton: Princeton Univ. Press, 1979.

Rose, Nikolas. "The Psychological Complex: Mental Measurement and Social Administration." *Ideology and Consciousness* 5 (Spring 1979), pp. 5–70.

Sadoul, Georges. *Histoire générale du cinéma.* 6 vols. 1948. Rpt. Paris: Denoel, 1973.

Sarduy, Severo. *Barroco.* Paris: Seuil, 1975.

Sartre, Jean-Paul. *The Family Idiot: Gustave Flaubert 1821–1857.* Trans. Carol Cosman. Chicago: Univ. of Chicago Press, 1981.

Sauvage, Leo. *L'affaire Lumière: Enquête sur les origines du cinéma.* Paris: Lherminier, 1985.

Schivelbusch, Wolfgang. *The Railway Journey: Trains and Travel in the 19th Century.* Trans. Anselm Hollo. New York: Urizen, 1979.

Schulz, Juergen. "Jacopo de'Barbari's View of Venice: Map Making and Moralized Geography Before the Year 1500." *Art Bulletin* 60 (1978), pp. 425–474.

Schwarz, Heinrich. *Art and Photography: Forerunners and Influences.* Chicago: Univ. of Chicago Press, 1985.

Sekula, Alan. *Photography Against the Grain: Essays and Photoworks 1973–1983.* Halifax: The Press of Nova Scotia College of Art and Design, 1984.

Sepper, Dennis L. *Goethe contra Newton: Polemics and the Project for a New Science of Color.* Cambridge: Univ. of Cambridge Press, 1988.

Serres, Michel. *La communication.* Paris: Minuit, 1969.

Serres, Michel. *La système de Leibniz et ses modelès mathématiques.* Paris: Presses Universitaires de France, 1968.

Serres, Michel. *La traduction.* Paris: Minuit, 1974.

Seymour, Charles Jr. "Dark Chamber and Light-Filled Room: Vermeer and the Camera Obscura." *Art Bulletin* 46, no. 3 (September 1964), pp. 323–331.

Silliman, R. H. "Fresnel and the Emergence of Physics as a Discipline." *Historical Studies in the Physical Sciences* 4 (1974), pp. 137–162.

Simmel, Georg. *The Philosophy of Money.* Trans. Tom Bottomore and David Frisby. London: Routledge and Kegan Paul, 1978.

Simon, Gérard. "A propos de la théorie de la perception visuelle chez Kepler et Descartes." In *Proceedings of XIIIth International Congress of the History of Science,* vol. 6, Moscow: Editions Naouka, 1974, pp. 237–245.

Simon, Gérard. *Le regard, l'être et l'apparence dans l'optique de l'antiquité.* Paris: Seuil, 1988.

Snyder, Joel. "Picturing Vision." *Critical Inquiry* 6 (Spring 1980), pp. 499–526.

Sternberger, Dolf. *Panorama of the Nineteenth Century*. New York: Urizen, 1977.

Tagg, John. "The Currency of Photography," In *Thinking Photography*. Ed. Victor Burgin. London: Macmillan, 1982.

Temkin, Oswei. "The Philosophical Background of Magendie's Physiology." *Bulletin of the History of Medicine* 20 (1946), pp. 10–27.

Tiedemann, Rolf. "Dialectics at a Standstill: Approaches to the Passagen-Werk." In *On Walter Benjamin: Critical Essays and Recollections*, ed. Gary Smith. Cambridge, Mass.: MIT Press, 1988.

Toulmin, Stephen. "The Inwardness of Mental Life," *Critical Inquiry* (Autumn 1979), pp. 1–16.

Turbayne, Colin Murray. *The Myth of Metaphor*. New Haven: Yale Univ. Press, 1962.

Vartanian, Aram. *Diderot and Descartes: A Study of Scientific Naturalism in the Enlightenment*. Princeton: Princeton Univ. Press, 1953.

Vattimo, Gianni. *The End of Modernity*. Trans. Jon R. Snyder. Baltimore: Johns Hopkins Univ. Press, 1988.

Virilio, Paul. *L'horizon négatif*. Paris: Galilée, 1984.

Wells, George A. "Goethe's Qualitative Optics." *The Journal of the History of Ideas* 32 (1971), pp. 617–626.

Wheelock, Arthur K. "Constantijn Huygens and Early Attitudes Toward the Camera Obscura." *History of Photography* 1, no. 2 (April 1977), pp. 93–101.

Wheelock, Arthur K. *Perspective, Optics, and Delft Artists Around 1650*. New York: Garland, 1977.

Wheelock, Arthur K. *Vermeer*. New York: Abrams, 1988.

White, Hayden. *Metahistory: The Historical Imagination in Nineteenth-Century Europe*. Baltimore: Johns Hopkins Univ. Press, 1973.

Wolman, Benjamin B. "The Historical Role of Johann Friedrich Herbart." In *Historical Roots of Contemporary Psychology*, ed. Benjamin B. Wolman. New York: Harper and Row, 1968, pp. 29–46.

Woodward, William R. "Fechner's Panpsychism: A Scientific Solution to the Mind-Body Problem." *Journal of the History of the Behavioral Sciences* 8 (October 1972), pp. 367–386.

Woodward, William R. "Hermann Lotze's Critique of Johannes Müller's Doctrine of Specific Sense." *Medical History* 19, no. 2 (April 1975), pp. 147–157.

Worringer, Wilhelm. *Abstraction and Empathy*. Trans. Michael Bullock. New York: International Universities Press, 1948.

Yolton, John W. *Perceptual Acquaintance from Descartes to Reid*. Minneapolis: Univ. of Minnesota Press, 1984.

Young, Robert M. *Mind, Brain, and Adaptation in the Nineteenth Century: Cerebral Localization and its Biological Context from Gall to Ferrier*. Oxford: Clarendon, 1970.

Index

Addison, Joseph, 64n84
Adorno, Theodor, 11, 57n69, 77, 132, 137
Aesthetics, 8, 12, 23, 75–76, 83–85, 116,
    143n15
Afterimage, retinal, 16, 21, 68–69, 97–98,
    100, 102–107, 118, 139–141, 142n12,
    146
Alberti, Leon Battista, 86. *See also*
    Perspective, Renaissance
Alhazen, 27
Alliez, Eric, 142n14
Alpers, Svetlana, 32n9, 34–36, 66n85
Ampère, André-Marie, 100
Analogy, 12, 37, 63
Anamorphosis, 33, 50n54
Angels, 142–143
Anschaulichkeit, 11
Antiquity, 17, 22, 93, 97
Arcades, 23
Architecture, 20, 39
    baroque, 51n56, 52n61
Aristotle, 27, 98
Art, 9, 11n11, 29, 34–36, 66, 83–84, 96,
    132, 137–138, 143n15. *See also*
    Cinema; Painting; Photography
    eighteenth-century, 52–54, 62–66
    historiography of, 3, 5, 21–23, 25–26,
    32–36, 149
    late antique, 22
    nineteenth-century, 3–4, 21–22, 96,
    116, 132, 138–143
    object, 5, 8, 21, 32
    seventeenth-century, 43–47
"Assemblages," 8, 30–32, 112, 126

Associationism, 57n72
Attention and attentiveness, 16, 18, 24, 84–
    85, 96, 102, 141, 149
Avant-garde, 3–4, 95–96, 126, 143n15

Babbage, Charles, 17n21
Bacon, Roger, 27
Barbari, Jacopo de', 52–53
    View of Venice, 53
Barthes, Roland, 129
Bataille, Georges, 147n20
Baudelaire, Charles, 20, 113–114, 116
Baudrillard, Jean, 11–12, 17n22
Behaviorism, 89n51, 100, 148
Bell, Sir Charles, 81, 89
Bellotto, Bernardo, 126
Benjamin, Walter, 11, 19–21, 23, 30n5, 112,
    127, 132
Bentham, Jeremy, 18
Bergson, Henri, 29, 72, 85n46, 89n53,
    98n2, 146
Berkeley, George, 39, 55, 57–58, 59, 62
Bernal, J. D., 131n50
Bernini, Gianlorenzo, 53n63
Bichat, Xavier, 78–79, 81, 89
Biology, 73, 77. *See also* Canguilhem,
    Georges; Physiology; Science
Blake, William, 70
Blindness, 58–60, 66. *See also* Molyneux
    problem
    caused by sun, 107, 141
Blind spot, 75, 104
Blumenberg, Hans, 50n55